The CLOUD of
WITNESSES
in the Courts of Heaven

Destiny Image Books by
Robert Henderson

Operating in the Courts of Heaven

Receiving Healing from the Courts of Heaven

Unlocking Destinies from the Courts of Heaven

Accessing the Courts of Heaven

*Prayers and Declarations that Open
the Courts of Heaven*

The Books of Heaven

The CLOUD of WITNESSES

in the Courts of Heaven

PARTNERING WITH THE COUNCIL OF HEAVEN
FOR PERSONAL AND KINGDOM BREAKTHROUGH

ROBERT HENDERSON

DESTINY IMAGE® PUBLISHERS, INC.
P.O. Box 310, Shippensburg, PA 17257-0310
"Promoting Inspired Lives."

This book and all other Destiny Image and Destiny Image Fiction books are available at Christian bookstores and distributors worldwide.

Cover design by Eileen Rockwell

For more information on foreign distributors, call 717-532-3040.

Reach us on the Internet: www.destinyimage.com.

ISBN 13 TP: 978-0-7684-4647-0

ISBN 13 eBook: 978-0-7684-4648-7

ISBN 13 HC: 978-0-7684-4650-0

ISBN 13 LP: 978-0-7684-4649-4

For Worldwide Distribution, Printed in the U.S.A.

1 2 3 4 5 6 7 8 / 23 22 21 20 19

Contents

Preface 7

Introduction 13

Chapter 1 Dimensions of the Spirit 19

Chapter 2 Shifts in the Spirit Realm 39

Chapter 3 Dead or Alive? 57

Chapter 4 One Church in Heaven and Earth 77

Chapter 5 Just and Perfected 99

Chapter 6 Reunifying Heaven and Earth 121

Chapter 7 Encountering the Cloud of Witnesses . . 141

Chapter 8 Jesus, the Mediator 159

Preface by Publisher

UP front, you need to know that this book tackles something that will surely be paradigm-stretching for some readers. At the same time, I do not believe that in any way, shape or form this work challenges traditional orthodox Christianity. In other words, author and apostolic leader, Robert Henderson presents this teaching with the intent of opening our spiritual eyes further to the activity in the invisible realm around us. His findings are heavily reinforced by Scripture.

Being a publisher of prophetic, Spirit-empowered resources, I've heard about the imbalances. I've experienced these firsthand, actually. Recently, I heard someone recount a testimony of his angelic encounter. I heard it shared on a video recording and something just didn't "sit right" with me about it. Discernment was kicking in and it provoked me to have a very honest conversation with the Lord.

"God, how do I know if these stories are for real? I believe people can have supernatural encounters, absolutely, but some of them don't sit well with me. Why?"

In this frustration-driven conversation, the Lord responded so clearly: "Those who have experienced the heavenly realm will carry a trembling on their lips when they recount it." Why? Everything in the heavenly realm, from the angels and heavenly host, to the Great Cloud of Witnesses, is marked by the weighty, majestic glory of God. All eyes are directed toward Jesus. None of these beings, although extraordinary, supernatural, and worth understanding, are deserving of worship or even an exaggerated focus. The gaze of that realm is fixed on the Lamb upon the throne.

When Robert teaches on the Cloud of Witnesses, I believe both his speech and his writing carry a trembling of the Lord. To read this book and interpret it as license to try and interact with "dead saints" is to miss the purpose entirely. Such would be a downright inappropriate, slopping interpretation of this book. We could never publish such a work or endorse such a heretical practice.

Why should we study about the Great Cloud of Witnesses (Hebrews 12:1-2) and the "spirits of just men made perfect? (Hebrews 12:23). Simple. It's important to understand, to the best of our ability, how different beings operate in the heavenly realm so that we here, on earth, can participate with their activity.

During a recent trip to Melbourne, Australia, I believe I had an encounter with the Great Cloud of Witnesses, particularly voices in the heavenly realm who interceded and contended on behalf of the nation of Australia. In the midst of a dynamic service where the speaker extended a powerful, "all-in" invitation for those present to give their everything to Jesus, I sensed unusual activity taking place in the spirit realm. God sovereignly opened up an awareness of the Cloud of Witnesses to me, specifically saints whose tears of intercession and bold activism shaped the faith landscape of Australia. I was undone by the reality that many of these heroes, like the unnamed ones listed in the latter section of Hebrews 11, died in faith. *Died in faith.* They did not die in doubt or die in wavering; they died in faith. I was overwhelmed by this thought. It's possible to die in faith when you don't live for the promise; you live for the Promiser. In this experience, two things took place. I was aware of the spirits of the just made perfect, who were operating in the Courts of Heaven as the Cloud of Witnesses. I was aware of their presence and activity, but within seconds, my gaze was immediately directed to the face of the Lord Jesus. Many of these witnesses could die in faith for one very clear reason: *they saw*

Him. A promise coming to pass, a prophecy fulfilled, or even a miracle manifesting was not their reward; Jesus was. This revelation filled my heart with awe, thus provoking me to lay my life down afresh for the Lord. *This is what happens when the Lord sovereignly brings us into these kinds of encounters.*

We don't ever pray to saints, angels or any heavenly being other than Father God. We don't set out to intentionally engage these experiences either. But when the Spirit of the Lord pulls back the veil, so to speak, and invites us into encounters with those in the heavenly dimension, we need to know how to steward such visitations. It's always for the purpose of propelling us further into our Kingdom assignment so that the Lamb will receive the reward of His suffering. Should one start to boast of their heavenly encounters or interactions with spiritual beings, this should provoke immediate concern. The chief end of supernatural encounters is not to supply us with stories to write books on or narratives that exalt our spirituality; encounters are meant to catalyze us into greater levels of fulfilling our assignment of advancing God's Kingdom on earth. One point that Robert reinforces throughout the book is that an increasing revelation of the Great Cloud of Witnesses further motivates us to lay down our lives for the cause of Christ, just as they all did.

Such will become increasingly normative. I know, it sounds weird and out of the box. But Jesus didn't place restrictions when He gave us the model prayer: "*Your kingdom come. Your will be done on earth as it is in heaven*" (See Matt. 6:8). The more "*on earth as it is in Heaven*" we experience, the more the invisible realm of Heaven will invade and impose upon the visible!

Read this book with an open heart and eyes fixed on Jesus. God sovereignly has the prerogative to usher you into whatever kind of encounter He deems fit that will encourage you lay down your life for Jesus and advance His Kingdom in a greater measure on earth.

—Larry Sparks
Publisher, Destiny Image

Introduction

IT seems in these times there is a revealing of certain mysteries that have been hidden. Or maybe it is a rediscovery of what our church ancestors knew but somehow forgot. One of these mysteries that is coming to the forefront is the Great Cloud of Witnesses. Perhaps because of the abuse of the idea in various cultures that worship the dead, talk to the dead, and other forms of interaction with the dead, we in the Western church have put up a wall against anything that sounds remotely similar. Just to be safe, we stay completely away from this concept.

Yet it would seem that the early church actually had a different view of these mysteries. The writer of Hebrews clearly tells us there is *"so great a cloud of witnesses"* that surrounds us. Hebrews 12:1 declares:

> *Therefore we also, since we are surrounded by **so great a cloud of witnesses,** let us lay*

aside every weight, and the sin which so easily ensnares us, and let us run with endurance the race that is set before us.

This would mean that these witnesses are not off on some distant place completely separated from the happenings on earth. If they surround us, they must be closer than we think, just in a different dimension or realm.

In my discussions with other ministry leaders concerning this idea, I find that many believe privately in encounters with the Cloud of Witnesses. They, however, choose not to talk about it publicly for fear of being misunderstood. Perhaps they are afraid that the Body of Christ is not mature enough to handle this and will go off on dangerous tangents with it. These days are now ended. It is definitely a supernatural idea to talk about the Cloud of Witnesses. I believe if the level of supernatural we have had would get the job done, we would have evangelized the world and seen a culture shift into Kingdom order a long time ago.

If we are going to truly see a demonstration of power, glory, and Kingdom authority that will sweep millions and even billions into the Kingdom of God, we must have new levels of the supernatural among us. This will involve the Great Cloud of Witnesses. As you will see as you continue reading this book, these witnesses can be used by God, along with angels, the Spirit of God, and other heavenly beings to influence and empower us for His purposes! We actually can work together to see the full intent of God done on the earth. This is at least partially what is meant in Hebrews 11:39-40:

> *And all these, having obtained a good testimony through faith, did not receive the promise,* **God** *having* **provided something better for us***, that they should not be made perfect apart from us.*

God has reserved a better thing for us as He has granted us the honor of co-laboring with these witnesses. Their perfection is dependent on us effectively working together. Even though they are in Heaven, they are waiting on something from us. You will find what I think this could be as you continue through this book.

As I have sensed and had encounters with this dimension, it always stirs me to lay my life down for God's will to be done instead of mine. Anything producing that devotion has to be considered as from the Lord. The devil and deceiving spirits are not going to motivate me to give up my life for the purpose of Jesus. They would want to drive me the other way in distraction. Every time I have had encounters with this realm, my heart is pressed to live a holier life for Jesus and to see His will done on earth.

Having said all this, I believe one thing is imperative. We are to always keep the first things first. The first thing first is Jesus. Paul told the Colossians in that book in chapter 2 verses 18 and 19 that they had to cling to Jesus:

> *Let no one cheat you of your reward, taking delight in false humility and worship of angels, intruding into those things which he has not seen, vainly puffed up by his fleshly mind, and not **holding fast** to the Head, from whom all the body, nourished and knit together by joints and ligaments, grows with the increase that is from God.*

Paul said that in the midst of all sorts of spiritual encounters that we must be *"holding fast"* to the Head of the Church—Jesus. We must never let go of Jesus to pursue other spiritual experiences. In fact, you will see throughout the book that we should not seek encounters with the Cloud of Witnesses. However, if in pursuit of Jesus and His purposes for our lives these encounters occur, we can trust them.

I hope to give you some insights and maybe even tools in this book to be aware of this dimension of the Great Cloud of Witnesses. Maybe, just maybe, they are closer and more involved than we have ever thought. God will help us to maintain our fundamentals while reaching into new places of the spiritual realm where the real things really are anyway. In Second Corinthians 4:18 it says what we see is temporary but what we don't see is eternal:

> *While we do not look at the things which are seen, but at the things which are not seen. For the things which are seen are temporary, but the things which are not seen are eternal.*

In addition to my insights and tools, four personal perspectives are included about godly supernatural encounters written by well-known and respected Christian ministry leaders: Mark Chironna, Patricia King, Kevin Zadai, and Ana Werner. Each reveals exciting truth about the spirit realm that will surely touch your heart, mind, and spirit.

There is a spirit realm we, by faith, must enter. This realm is eternal and controls this natural realm. God is inviting us to encounter the realm He Himself lives in. Let's say yes to Him and make ourselves available. Maybe in the pursuit of Jesus we might awaken to things we've not known before. Please enjoy this book.

Chapter 1

Dimensions of the Spirit

ONE of our greatest challenges as believers is believing in the unseen realm. When you stop to think about it, it seems crazy that this would be such a challenge. As Christians our belief system is rooted in the understanding that the unseen dimension influences and even controls the seen realm. Yet if we allow nature to take its course, we allow the natural world to dominate our view of life. There is, however, a very real spiritual dimension that is unseen by most. This realm has to be entered by faith. As extraordinary as this may seem, we all actually have the ability to function there. Hebrews 12:22-24 accurately describes a spiritual, unseen dimension we are called to and have already come to:

> *But you have **come to** Mount Zion and to the city of the living God, the heavenly Jerusalem, to an innumerable company of angels, to the general assembly and church of the firstborn who*

are registered in heaven, to God the Judge of all,
to the spirits of just men made perfect, to Jesus
the Mediator of the new covenant, and to the
blood of sprinkling that speaks better things than
that of Abel.

This Scripture lists many things we have been granted access into in the spirit realm. Most of the time we would see Scriptures like these and place them in a *theological statement* category. I, however, think this is a mistake. These kinds of Scriptures are not just theological statements, they are to be *spiritual experiences*. The writer of Hebrews is seeking to express to us activity in the spiritual unseen realm we should expect to encounter. When it declares we have *come to* these, it is unveiling operations and functions of a heavenly realm. Because we have *come to* them, there is the implication that we are in the spirit realm where they are. This is not just a theological statement or brainteaser. This is to be a spiritual experience and even encounter in these dimensions.

To really appreciate this concept, we should realize that the book of Hebrews is a very mystical book. The term "mystical" might scare some believers. Collins Dictionary lists the definition of "mystical" as relating to or based on intuition, contemplation, or meditation of a spiritual nature. It also can involve that which is mysterious. Wikipedia describes "mysticism" as the practice of religious ecstasies, together with whatever ideologies, ethics, rites, myths, legends, and magic may be related to them.

When I think of something being mystical, I think of it being super-spiritual for today's Church. Yet the book of Hebrews, which was accepted into the canon of Scripture, makes some pretty mystical claims. It speaks of angels, unseen priesthoods, blood that is speaking, a celestial Judge, a Mediator securing salvation, and a company of people who have died yet are still alive in a heavenly dimension. When we look from this perspective, it can seem really challenging to the level of spirituality of most believers today.

However, I believe it is God's intent to bring the Church into a new level of spirituality. If we are not careful, we will reduce our experience down to only what can be explained logically. This will produce in us what Paul warned Timothy of in Second Timothy 3:5 concerning the last days and the people of that era:

Having a form of godliness but denying its
power. And from such people turn away!

I take this to mean we look religious, sound religious, and seem religious, but there is no power associated with us. John G. Lake, the great minister who shook South Africa with the healing power of God and formed the healing rooms in Spokane, Washington, that allowed it to be declared the healthiest city in America in his day said, "Christianity is not a philosophy, it is a power." He further stated this is what sets Christianity apart from every other religion. At our core, we believe our Founder, after being brutally beaten and mutilated to the point of being unrecognizable, rose from the dead and is now in Heaven standing on our behalf. This is pretty mystical when you stop and think about it.

Our problem is, traditional Christianity has made us consider anything that has a twinge of mysticism attached to it as weird and to even be afraid of it. This has kept us bound with logic, intellectualism, and rationale rather than being the supernatural people we are to be. Again, the book of Hebrews implies that we are this kind of people. Hebrews 2:11-13 speaks of us and Jesus being joined in a spiritual connection:

> *For both He who sanctifies and those who are being sanctified are all of one, for which reason* **He is not ashamed to call them brethren**, *saying: "I will declare Your name to My brethren; in the midst of the assembly I will sing praise to You." And again: "I will put My trust in Him." And again: "Here am I and the children whom God has given Me."*

This speaks of us having the same DNA as Jesus. In the natural, what makes people siblings is having the same parents. This is what results in the same or similar DNA being in those who are related. You and I have the same stuff in us as Jesus. We have the divine nature of God in us. The same nature of God in Jesus is now in us. Jesus is therefore not ashamed to call us His brothers and sisters. Notice the last part of the Scripture mentions that we are also His children whom God gave to Him.

The following is from Isaiah 8:18 that further explains the DNA that is part of us by our new birth:

Here am I and the children whom the Lord has given me! We are for signs and wonders in Israel from the Lord of hosts, who dwells in Mount Zion.

As children who carry the same DNA as Jesus, both as His siblings but also as children given to Him by God, we are created for signs and wonders. We are made for the supernatural. We must stop denying who we are and embrace these dimensions and realities. Part of this supernatural realm we are to walk in is described in the Hebrews verses previously mentioned. We are meant to walk among all the spiritual activity mentioned in this realm.

The first thing mentioned is we have come to Mount Zion. This is the name of the dimension of the spirit we have come to. Everything mentioned after that is the activity of that dimension. We will get into this so we can see that the Great Cloud of Witnesses is part of a major operation from the heavenly realm. Mount Zion is a dimension of the spiritual realm. Clearly when we read that we have come to Mount Zion, the writer is not speaking of boarding a plane and flying to Israel. Coming to Mount Zion is speaking of stepping into a supernatural realm where all sorts of heavenly activity is occurring. Mount Zion is several things in the spirit realm. It is the place of His presence. Psalm 76:1-2 tells us that God dwells in Zion:

> *In Judah God is known; His name is great in Israel. In Salem also is His tabernacle, and His dwelling place in Zion.*

One of the ways we know we have come to Mount Zion, is that we suddenly sense His presence in the atmosphere. This is because He dwells in Zion. Psalm 132:13 tells us that God has chosen Zion as the place of His habitation:

> *For the Lord has chosen Zion; He has desired it for His dwelling place.*

There are many different ways to discern what is happening in the spiritual realm. One can see, hear, feel, smell (discern), and even taste. All five of the natural senses have spiritual correlations. I have experienced all five of these means of deciding what is occurring in the spirit realm. I, however, am much more of a hearer and a feeler. I can sense or tell when I have stepped into Mount Zion in the spirit world because I *feel* the atmosphere change. I become aware of His presence and of His closeness. This is because He has chosen Zion as His desired place of habitation. When I sense this, I know I am now standing among varied heavenly activity.

Another characteristic of Mount Zion is it is a place of government. When we step into Mount Zion, we are moving into a place where our activity does more than change things concerning just us. Our activities in this realm can actually alter cultures and shift nations. Psalm 110:1-2 shows that the rod of God's strength comes out of Zion:

> The Lord said to my Lord, "Sit at My right hand, till I make Your enemies Your footstool." The Lord shall send the rod of Your strength out of Zion. Rule in the midst of Your enemies!

From this spiritual realm called Mount Zion, God sends forth His rulership through us. This means that a Kingdom manifestation begins to be seen on the earth. God through us from Zion begins to rule in the midst of His enemies. Out from the place of His habitation and presence, His authority is manifested and seen. Another part of Mount Zion that we step into is a resting place. Psalm 132:13-14 says:

> *For the Lord has chosen Zion; He has desired it*
> *for His dwelling place: "This is My resting place*
> *forever; here I will dwell, for I have desired it."*

When we step into Zion as a spiritual dimension, we step into God's resting place. This is important because *rest* is a dimension of the spirit in and of itself. Hebrews 4:9-11 speaks of a place of rest in the spirit world:

> *There remains therefore a rest for the people of*
> *God. For he who has entered His rest has himself*
> *also ceased from his works as God did from His.*
> *Let us therefore be diligent to enter that rest, lest*
> *anyone fall according to the same example of*
> *disobedience.*

There is a rest that God is still waiting for a people to move into. In this place of rest, we no longer strive in our own efforts. Everything is done through the impetus of the Holy Spirit. Rest is not just a place of quietness. Rest is a place of rulership. When we step into this realm of Zion, from this dimension a whisper can change nations. Jesus is sitting in perfect rest at the right hand of the Father. Hebrews 10:12-13 declares He is waiting until His enemies are subdued and become His footstool:

> *But this Man, after He had offered one sacrifice for sins forever, sat down at the right hand of God, from that time waiting till His enemies are made His footstool.*

Jesus is confident in His sacrifice and work. He is now waiting until His people, His Church, take all He has done and subdue every enemy under His feet. He is at rest! When we step into this same arena of rest, from this place all enemies are subdued. The Lord is teaching us how to operate out of Zion from this place of the rest of the Lord.

Within Mount Zion are all kinds of spiritual activity. As we move into this place we have *come to*, we can encounter and agree with this realm. Joshua, the High Priest in Zechariah 3:7, was told he could walk among this activity:

> *Thus says the Lord of hosts: "If you will walk in My ways, and if you will keep My command, then you shall also judge My house, and likewise*

> *have charge of My courts; I will give you places*
> *to walk among these who stand here."*

As High Priest, Joshua was being granted access into this realm where all this heavenly activity was happening. He was being given the right to function here in agreement with what was occurring in the spirit realm. So have we as New Covenant kings and priests. Other Scriptures, for example Hebrews 12:22-24, tell us what activity is going on in Mount Zion. We have come to the heavenly city, New Jerusalem. We know that the heavenly city is the bride of the Lord. Revelation 21:9-10 shows us this city coming out of Heaven, which is the bride of the Lamb:

> *Then one of the seven angels who had the seven*
> *bowls full of the seven last plagues came and said*
> *to me, "Come, I will show you the bride, the*
> *Lamb's wife." And he carried me away in the*
> *Spirit to a great, high mountain, and showed me*
> *the great city, the holy Jerusalem, descending out*
> *of heaven from God.*

This bride that is a city, which is a people, the Church, is in perfect union with the Lord. Galatians 4:26 shows she is the lover of the Lord, but is also the *mother of us all:*

But the Jerusalem above is free, which is the mother of us all.

In other words, the bride's union with Jesus as the Bridegroom causes conception and birthing of things onto the earth. We have *come to* and are part of this bride who conceives and gives birth. We carry in intercession and travail the passions and purposes of the Lord to full term. We then birth His pleasure on the earth. We have come to this people that is this city in the spirit realm.

We have also *come to* an innumerable and festal company of angels. As we step into these dimensions of the spirit, we enter the territory of angels. They are helpers and messengers of God. They are also to minister to the heirs of salvation. Hebrews 1:13-14 says they are here to minister to us who are receivers of salvation:

But to which of the angels has He ever said: "Sit at My right hand, till I make Your enemies Your footstool"? Are they not all ministering spirits sent forth to minister for those who will inherit salvation?

Angels are here to help us, empower us, and work in agreement with us for God's purposes. We have *come to* this dimension where they are.

We have also *come to* the governmental people of God called the Church. This people are registered in Heaven. This means they are recognized. They have a right to stand before the Lord in His Courts and council and petition Him even on behalf of nations. We are part of this company. This company is made up of what is on earth and in Heaven. Ephesians 3:14-15 tells us the whole family is named and recognized by the Father:

> *For this reason I bow my knees to the Father of our Lord Jesus Christ, from whom the whole family in heaven and earth is named.*

The interesting thing to me here is that God recognizes both who is in Heaven and who is on earth as part of the family called the Church. It takes both the heavenly and the earthly working together to constitute the Church. We on earth must learn to recognize the heavenly and move in agreement with it. The Church is not just what is on earth. It also includes what is in Heaven. When Heaven and earth agree together, the earth is changed!

We have also *come to* God the Judge of all. As Judge, decisions are rendered because of our activity before Him in the council and the Courts of Heaven. We can petition the Lord in His position as Judge and see these decisions released that causes life to shift on the planet. Judges only render verdicts as a result of testimony presented. As we come to stand in this place called Mount Zion, we present cases and information that allow the passion of the Judge to be fulfilled.

We have also *come to* the spirit of just men and women made perfect. This is a reference to the Great Cloud of Witnesses. We will discuss this in more depth in a later chapter.

We have *come* as well to Jesus the Mediator of the New Covenant. Through His intercession for us, we are able to enter into all that He died for us to have. Hebrews 7:25 says He ever lives to intercede:

> *Therefore He is also able to save to the uttermost those who come to God through Him, since He always lives to make intercession for them.*

Jesus not only died for us, He is ever praying to see that we move into the full benefit of it. Jesus, and His intercession as our Mediator and High Priest, is the means to fully experience all that He provided for us from His sacrifice. We have *come to* the blood of sprinkling that is speaking for us. Just like Abel's blood cried out against Cain after Cain killed him, the blood of Jesus is crying out for us and our redemption. The blood of Jesus is releasing testimony on our behalf, giving God the legal right He needs to forgive us.

God has always had a heart and desire to forgive. He, however, needs a legal right to do it from. This is why in the Old Testament the priest had to offer the blood of bulls and goats. The *testimony* of that blood gave God the legal right to remove their sins from them for a year. Hebrews 10:1-4 shows us that this yearly offering of the Passover lamb could only grant the people a reprieve from judgment on a yearly basis:

> *For the law, having a shadow of the good things to come, and not the very image of the things, can never with these same sacrifices, which they offer continually year by year, make those who approach perfect. For then would they not have ceased to be offered? For the worshipers, once purified, would have had no more consciousness of sins. But in those sacrifices there is a reminder of sins every year. For it is not possible that the blood of bulls and goats could take away sins.*

Not only did these sacrifices only suffice for a year, but they were a reminder of their sins from year to year. The people lived with a perpetual sense of guilt and shame. The blood of Jesus, however, doesn't just cover and atone for our sins for a year—it cleanses them away forever. Hebrews 9:14 says that the blood of Jesus purges our conscience of the guilt and stain of sin. We are able to live our lives with a God consciousness and not a sin consciousness.

> *How much more shall the blood of Christ, who through the eternal Spirit offered Himself without spot to God, cleanse your conscience from dead works to serve the living God?*

We no longer live our lives under condemnation and guilt, but rather as new creations who have been cleansed from all our dead works! This is because the blood of Jesus is speaking for us and granting God the legal right to completely forgive and cleanse us.

This is what is in the spiritual dimension we have *come to*. We by faith agree with and attach ourselves to all that is functioning on our behalf in this realm. We will see in the coming chapters how the Great Cloud of Witnesses is connected to all this heavenly activity and is part of it.

In the ninth article of the Apostle's Creed, we confess, "I believe in the Communion of Saints." This is part of the Christian "Tradition" with a capitol T.

The word "tradition" has become demonized progressively in the post-modern era, because the very mantra of the post-modern era is "There are no absolutes"—which, ironically, is an "absolute" statement that is therefore self-contradictory.

The post-modern era has questioned everything that preceded it and is responsible for calling into question every area of society where there are "institutions" (including the Church). Sadly, in a highly secular culture, the Church has bought into that line of thinking. The 12 Articles of the Apostle's Creed are as relevant now as when they were recited by those being baptized in the early Church, including the doctrine of the Communion of Saints.

What exactly is the doctrine of the Communion of Saints? Very simply, it is threefold: 1) our communion as believers with the Triune God; 2) our communion with the Church Triumphant (the saints who have already gone on to their reward); and 3) our communion with the Church Militant (the saints on earth who continue to fight the good fight of faith while in their present earthly existence). The Communion of the Saints as an article of the Creed is not something dead and dry. In fact, it is an indication of the fervor and conviction of the early Church in their conviction of the mystical union between Christ and His Church, both on earth and in Heaven.

Robert Henderson tells some very powerful accounts of encounters he has experienced while asleep, that might for some sound strange and radical. However, a careful study of Church history, from its ancient origins until even now, reveals that what Robert has experienced is more common than we might have thought or realized. Encounters with those who have joined the Cloud of Witnesses in Heaven and have passed out of this life into the next are testified to throughout Church history.

Athanasius (AD 293-AD 373), who was the Bishop of Alexandria, also known as Athanasius the Confessor, one of the great Ante-Nicene Fathers and doctors of the Church, was the chief defender of Christian orthodoxy in the 4th Century against the heresy known as Arianism. While he experienced persecution by four Roman Emperors during his 45-year tenure as Bishop of Alexandria, it is his writings that gave shape to the future of the Church.

Arianism is the belief that Jesus was "created" by God. This heresy had spread through the entire Church. It challenged the very revelation of the Triune Godhead—Father, Son, and Spirit—as revealed in the Sacred Text through Christ Himself. Athanasius was the key voice to the hammering out of the nature of "three Persons in one substance" in speaking of the Triune God.

This is important to know and substantiates the scholarship and the commitment Athanasius had to the Gospel. He penned these words among many others: *"Those who maintain 'There was a time when the Son was not' rob God of his Word, like plunderers."* "Word" here is not Scripture, "Word" here is the Logos Himself, the Second Person of the Godhead, God of very God as it says in the Nicene Creed.

It is this great doctor and scholar of the Church, deeply committed and devoted to Christ, who in his own experience with the Triune life of the Godhead would say these words about the Communion of the Saints in His treatise, *Against the Heathen:*

…When the body lies in bed, not moving, but in death-like sleep, the soul keeps awake by virtue of its own power, and transcends the natural power of the body, and as though traveling away from the body while remaining in it, imagines and beholds things above the earth, and often even holds converse with the saints and angels who are above earthly and bodily existence, and approaches them in the confidence of the purity of its intelligence; shall it not all the more, when separated from the body at the time appointed by God Who coupled them together, have its knowledge of immortality more clear? For if even when coupled with the body it lived a life outside the body, much more shall its life continue after the death of the body, and live without ceasing by reason of God Who made it thus by His own Word, our Lord Jesus Christ.

The intent by those who believe that all things miraculous ceased with the completion of the Canon by the late 4th Century, is all too common in Western Evangelicalism. While the doctrine of the Communion of the Saints would not necessarily be a part of the argument against the ongoing demonstration of the Spirit in signs and wonders, because of the mystical nature of these kinds of experiences, it all-too-often is reduced to rational, scientific, Enlightenment explanations by those who essentially take the cessationist perspective.

Robert Henderson, transparently and genuinely shares experiences he has had, in relation to the Communion of the Saints, not unlike Bishop Athanasius of Alexandria, and many, many others in the ancient Church, and throughout Church history. He is inviting you, in this book, to be aware that indeed, these kinds of experiences continue to happen in our lives, often when we least expect them to.

Robert speaks in clear and plain tones and makes his experiences accessible to all of us. *The Cloud of*

Witnesses in the Courts of Heaven is written for the everyday person who is walking with the everyday God and Father of our Lord Jesus Christ, through the fellowship of the Holy Spirit.

—Dr. Mark J. Chironna
Church on the Living Edge
Mark Chironna Ministries
Longwood, Florida

Chapter 2

Shifts in the Spirit Realm

I have often wondered what transpires in the spirit realm when someone dies. The Bible gives us insight into this by some of the terms used to describe death and stepping into the afterlife. For instance, God told Josiah in Second Chronicles 34:28 that he would be gathered to his ancestors and would not see the evil that would come on the land:

> "Surely I will gather you to your fathers, and you shall be gathered to your grave in peace; and your eyes shall not see all the calamity which I will bring on this place and its inhabitants." So they brought back word to the king.

This speaks of a great reunion occurring with those who have died before us. Of course, we are speaking of this from a Christian perspective and those who are born again and saved. When we die we will encounter those who have died before us. There will be a gathering together again with our loved ones who know the Lord.

The Bible also gives us further insight in the story Jesus told of Lazarus and the rich man in Luke 16:22. Lazarus was a beggar while there was a rich man who lived in opulence. Both died. The Bible describes Lazarus' transition to Heaven:

> *So it was that the beggar died, and was carried by the angels to Abraham's bosom. The rich man also died and was buried.*

Angels came and carried the rich man to be with Abraham in paradise. It would appear that when those who belong to God die, there is an angelic escort into our heavenly dwelling places. We do not make the journey by ourselves. Such suggests that the angels of God help us and carry us into this next place of our existence.

Another term that is used to express this transition from this life to the next one is found in Second Timothy 4:6:

> *For I am already being poured out as a drink offering, and the time of my departure is at hand.*

The word "departure" is the Greek word *analusis* and among other things it means to raise the anchor for a ship to sail away. This would imply that while we are here in our natural bodies we are anchored. We are tied off and are not free to sail into the vast unknowns. At death, however, we become untethered. The anchor is raised and we are freed from the restrictions of this mortal flesh. We are freed in the spirit to move in a way not known until then. This is an amazing picture for us of the glory of the next life as opposed to the fear of death.

Paul also spoke of the next realm of life in First Corinthians 13:8-12 when he described what we know now in contrast to what and how we will know then:

> *Love never fails. But whether there are prophecies, they will fail; whether there are tongues, they will cease; whether there is knowledge, it will vanish away. For we know in part and we prophesy in part. But when that which is perfect has come, then that which is in part will be done away. When I was a child, I spoke as a child, I understood as a child, I thought as a child; but when I became a man, I put away childish things. For now we see in a mirror, dimly, but then face to face. Now I know in part, but then I shall know just as I also am known.*

Paul is describing the next life in comparison to this one. In the next life there will be no need of prophecy, tongues are knowledge. The only thing that will remain is love. Everything in part will be done away with because the complete will have come. Clearly the complete is love. First John 4:8 tells us that God Himself is love:

> *He who does not love does not know God, for God is love.*

As it is reported, when the prophet Bob Jones was allowed to visit Heaven before he was sent back to earth, he understood the question we would be asked in judgment to be, "Did you learn to love?" It appears that the overriding value of Heaven is love.

Paul went on to liken this life to being a child. He writes of speaking as a child, thinking as a child, and reasoning as a child. This is what we do in this life in comparison to being an adult in the next life. Our speech, thoughts, and reasoning will be advanced in the next life much like the difference between a child and an adult is in this life. There will be a new level of awareness and maturity.

He then likens this life to seeing in a mirror dimly. The next life in comparison will be like standing face to face. In other words, in this life it is like seeing a reflection that you can't embrace. In the next life there will be the full substance of what we can hold.

Paul then speaks of us knowing only partly in this life. There are unknowns we have no answer for in this life. In the next life, however, we will know fully. All questions will be answered. We will also be fully known. I think this means we will have a full sense of our identity and who we are. Paul spoke of this in Colossians 3:4:

> *When Christ who is our life appears, then you*
> *also will appear with Him in glory.*

When Jesus is revealed and we step into the next life, we shall also be revealed with Him. A full awareness of who we are shall be seen by us and everyone. First John 3:1-3 tells us that who we really are will not be fully known until Jesus appears:

> *Behold what manner of love the Father has*
> *bestowed on us, that we should be called children*
> *of God! Therefore the world does not know us,*
> *because it did not know Him. Beloved, now*
> *we are children of God; and it has not yet been*
> *revealed what we shall be, but we know that*
> *when He is revealed, we shall be like Him, for*
> *we shall see Him as He is. And everyone who*

*has this hope in Him purifies himself, just as He
is pure.*

The world does not know who we are. Therefore, we should not allow the world to tell us who we are or to fashion and form us. We are told that what we shall be has not been fully seen. It will only be manifest when we see Him. In other words, we shall be fully known. All the searching for identity and significance will be over. A full revelation of who we are will be set in place. As those who have this hope, it should birth in us a desire to be pure before Him. We allow the purifying work of God to move in us and through us in the hope of fully becoming like Him. In the next life we will know even as we are known.

The passing from this life to the next should be a very exciting time. The apostle Paul had no fear of this. In fact, he had an expectation of this time when it occurred. Philippians 1:21-25 shows Paul wrestling with going on to Heaven or staying here on earth. It would appear that perhaps God was giving him a choice:

*For to me, to live is Christ, and to die is gain.
But if I live on in the flesh, this will mean fruit
from my labor; yet what I shall choose I cannot
tell. For I am hard-pressed between the two,
having a desire to depart and be with Christ,*

which is far better. Nevertheless to remain in
the flesh is more needful for you. And being
confident of this, I know that I shall remain and
continue with you all for your progress and joy
of faith.

Paul chooses to stay on earth for the benefit of the Church and God's people who needed him. He, however, was aware that dying was gain. He knew the next life was far better than this one. We will step into the next life with perhaps an even greater influence. It is said of Abel in Hebrews 11:4, who offered a more excellent sacrifice, that he being dead is still speaking:

By faith Abel offered to God a more excellent
sacrifice than Cain, through which he obtained
witness that he was righteous, God testifying of
his gifts; and through it he being dead still speaks.

In my estimation, this does not just mean that the life Abel lived is still impacting today, even though that is true. I believe that the life Abel lived granted him status in Heaven. His position in Heaven as part of the Great Cloud of Witnesses is still allowing him to have impact today. God witnessing and testifying of his righteousness because of the gifts he brought secured for him this place of influence in the heavenly realm.

What we do in this life does determine our place in the next life and the realm of Heaven. We can see something of this from Isaiah 6:1:

> *In the year that King Uzziah died, I saw the*
> *Lord sitting on a throne, high and lifted up, and*
> *the train of His robe filled the temple.*

What was there about the death of Uzziah that unlocked a new spiritual dimension that allowed this encounter for Isaiah? Isaiah is already a prophet of the Lord, yet he connects the dying of Uzziah to his experience in the glory of God and His throne room. Was Isaiah just using the death of Uzziah as a timeline to pinpoint for the reader when this visitation occurred? I don't think so.

Or was Isaiah suggesting that the dying of Uzziah unlocked something in the spirit realm that allowed him to have this encounter that wasn't allowed before? For instance, for decades it has been declared that when Reverend Billy Graham died there would be a new visitation of God on earth. His death would release a great move of God that would produce waves of evangelism and power. This would cause millions if not a billion souls to be swept into the Kingdom. The idea is what Jesus spoke of in John 12:24:

> *Most assuredly, I say to you, unless a grain of wheat falls into the ground and dies, it remains alone; but if it dies, it produces much grain.*

Jesus, in referring to Himself, said that as He died, the result would be a massive reproducing of disciples like Him who carried the same power and authority. This is exactly what happened. Jesus' death caused a multiplication of Himself on the earth. Just like a grain of wheat is put into the ground and germinates, it causes a multiplication and harvest to occur. Jesus is declaring this is the same principle of harvest that would take place at His death. John 14:12 states that Jesus ascending to the Father and sending the Holy Spirit would cause even greater demonstration through the disciples:

> *Most assuredly, I say to you, he who believes in Me, the works that I do he will do also; and greater works than these he will do, because I go to My Father.*

There would be a multiplying of supernatural works that would take place through the disciples because Jesus died, was resurrected, and went to the

Father. Unless Jesus allowed this process to happen, He would have been just one man with great but limited effect. However, because He chose to die and lay His life down, it released a harvest of those who for 2,000 years plus have been changing the world. Hebrews 2:10 shows that through Jesus' suffering, as the captain of our salvation, many sons and daughters of glory would be produced:

> *For it was fitting for Him, for whom are all things and by whom are all things, in bringing many sons to glory, to make the captain of their salvation perfect through sufferings.*

Jesus' life being given as a seed in the ground has allowed the harvest and impact of His life to be greatly expanded. This is the idea concerning Billy Graham. Many believe that when he died naturally, that his life became a seed that will produce a massive harvest of evangelism and souls. As a result of who he is, his death would allow this.

When I look at what Isaiah said about Uzziah, I have to consider that maybe the same thing occurred with him. I think it is clear that Uzziah's death caused something in the spirit world to be opened that was closed until that time. It seems very apparent to me that Uzziah's death shifted something in the unseen realm.

We are still seeing this today, especially on the negative side. For instance, when magazine publisher Hugh Hefner died, who was a propagator of lust, uncleanness, and all manner of sin and immorality, something shifted. Within weeks if not days of Hefner's death, film producer Harvey Weinstein was exposed in Hollywood for his abuse and scandalous behavior with women. That which had been known behind the scenes for decades was suddenly uncovered. Then the process and accusations of many high-profile men and their abuse and mistreatment of women sexually began to be revealed. Why did this happen right after the death of Hugh Hefner, the founder of *Playboy* magazine? The answer is, his death resulted in movement in the spirit world. It seems that the principalities and powers that rule over even nations are empowered by human activity and agreement. Ephesians 6:12 gives some insight to this:

> *For we do not wrestle against flesh and blood, but against principalities, against powers, against the rulers of the darkness of this age, against spiritual hosts of wickedness in the heavenly places.*

There are powers of darkness that actually influence the culture of nations. From their position in the heavenly realms or the unseen realms of the spirit, they influence the minds of people. Second

Corinthians 10:4-6 describes some of the conflict we are in for the minds of culture:

> *For the weapons of our warfare are not carnal*
> *but mighty in God for pulling down strongholds,*
> *casting down arguments and every high thing*
> *that exalts itself against the knowledge of God,*
> *bringing every thought into captivity to the obe-*
> *dience of Christ, and being ready to punish all*
> *disobedience when your obedience is fulfilled.*

This is not just describing a personal battle to control our minds, but actually is describing the battle for a culture's mind. We are told that we can bring down arguments, high things seeking to exalt themselves, and every thought process that is operating in a culture. One of the ways to do this is through removing the principalities' empowerment that is coming from humans. The reason humans empower powers of darkness is because God gave the earth realm to humankind. Psalm 115:16 tells us that the domain of the earth is under men:

> *The heaven, even the heavens, are the Lord's;*
> *but the earth He has given to the children of*
> *men.*

As a result of humans having charge and the authority in the earthly realm, who they choose to empower, they are empowered. When humans set their hearts and wills toward the heavenly, Heaven is empowered on earth. However, when humans set their hearts and wills toward the demonic, the demonic is empowered.

When satan put into the heart of Hugh Hefner to create *Playboy* magazine and he did, it brought an empowerment to that demon of lust and uncleanness over nations. It unlocked a torrent of filth and pollution that has defiled millions if not billions. However, when Hefner died, the principality power was reduced, because the one who empowered him was now removed. The result has been the uncovering of all sorts of wickedness in very high places. Exposures have come because the powers of darkness that propagated and covered them was now removed. This all happened because someone died and their death shifted something in the spiritual dimension. This is on the demonic side. It also occurs in the positive.

When King Uzziah died, something that had been closed opened. Isaiah encountered the glory of God's presence in a powerful way. What was it about Uzziah's death that caused this spiritual realm to open that had been closed to that point? King Uzziah was a good king who got off track and acted presumptuously.

Second Chronicles 26:3-4 tells us that Uzziah did good and right as king before the Lord:

> *Uzziah was sixteen years old when he became king, and he reigned fifty-two years in Jerusalem. His mother's name was Jecholiah of Jerusalem. And he did what was right in the sight of the Lord, according to all that his father Amaziah had done.*

God was pleased with Uzziah. However, after much success and blessing of the Lord, Uzziah didn't guard his heart. Second Chronicles 26:16-21 tells us a sad story of a mighty king who through an act of presumption didn't end well:

> *But when he was strong his heart was lifted up, to his destruction, for he transgressed against the Lord his God by entering the temple of the Lord to burn incense on the altar of incense. So Azariah the priest went in after him, and with him were eighty priests of the Lord—valiant men. And they withstood King Uzziah, and said to him, "It is not for you, Uzziah, to burn incense to the Lord, but for the priests, the sons of Aaron, who are consecrated to burn incense. Get out of the sanctuary, for you have tres-*

passed! You shall have no honor from the Lord God."

Then Uzziah became furious; and he had a censer in his hand to burn incense. And while he was angry with the priests, leprosy broke out on his forehead, before the priests in the house of the Lord, beside the incense altar. And Azariah the chief priest and all the priests looked at him, and there, on his forehead, he was leprous; so they thrust him out of that place. Indeed he also hurried to get out, because the Lord had struck him.

King Uzziah was a leper until the day of his death. He dwelt in an isolated house, because he was a leper; for he was cut off from the house of the Lord. Then Jotham his son was over the king's house, judging the people of the land.

The Lord struck Uzziah because of his presumption to operate as a priest. This was not allowed in the day. He was king but was not priest. Only in New Testament order are we allowed to operate as both kings and priests to our God (see Revelation 1:6). This is part of the New Testament blessing. In the Old Testament, only David, who had this revelation as an Old Testament man, was allowed this privilege. When Uzziah tried to do it, it was a severe miscalculation of judgment. He was penalized harshly. This resulted in the king being a leper until he died and having to turn rulership over to his son.

It could be that something happened in the spirit realm as a result of this disobedience. A spiritual dimension of glory was shut and sealed because of King Uzziah's trespass. Could it be that the devil, our adversary, used the king's sin as a legal right to deny access into this glorious realm of the spirit? It appears that something shut it down until the death of Uzziah. When his death occurred, the legal right of the devil to have this dimension closed to Isaiah was removed. Isaiah was now free to have this encounter with God.

One other thought I want to share here could be even more radical. What if Uzziah, when he transitioned into the heavenly realm at his death, actually petitioned the Lord to open this realm to Isaiah? The Bible says those who laid their lives down for the purposes of the Kingdom of God are given a place in the Cloud of Witnesses (Hebrews 11:39). This is a place of great influence in Heaven. Perhaps Uzziah, because of his previous life before the transgression, had a status in Heaven that he could speak from. Could it be that his petitions allowed the realm that had been closed to Isaiah as a prophet to open up? I am not saying Isaiah *prayed* to Uzziah. No! No! No! A thousand times no! I am saying that perhaps Uzziah out of his own passion asked the Lord as part of the Great Cloud of Witnesses to please open this realm.

Perhaps people dying and going into the heavenly realm as part of the Cloud of Witnesses gives us new places of power before the throne of God. The result is new heavenly activity and encounter of Heaven for us on earth. The Great Cloud of Witnesses are giving testimony on our behalf before the throne, in agreement with Jesus' intercession. Their witness before the throne calls us into remembrance before God.

This is just a thought concerning the activity of those who die and enter this realm. Perhaps they are doing more than we know. Perhaps they actually are still helping the process of the Kingdom from where they are. May the Lord grant us wisdom and understanding.

Chapter 3

Dead or Alive?

IN my lifetime I have been aware of a shift in the mindset and thinking concerning the Cloud of Witnesses. I'm sure there were those in times past who had a revelation of this dimension in the spirit. It seems now, however, that there is an interest and even increased encounters with these witnesses.

When we speak of the Great Cloud of Witnesses, we are talking of those who have already transitioned into Heaven. They are presently in a heavenly realm with a function to still see God's will done. Hebrews 12:1-2 give us the foundational understanding of this realm:

> *Therefore we also, since we are surrounded by so **great a cloud of witnesses,** let us lay aside every weight, and the sin which so easily ensnares us, and let us run with endurance the race that is set before us, looking unto Jesus,*

the author and finisher of our faith, who for the
joy that was set before Him endured the cross,
despising the shame, and has sat down at the
right hand of the throne of God.

These verses come on the heels of Hebrews chapter 11 where the people of faith who changed the world are spoken of with great admiration. These are obviously some of those who are part of this great cloud. The latter portion of Hebrews records some intriguing ideas for us concerning those who lived faithfully. Hebrews 11:37-40 reveal insight into their past and present function:

They were stoned, they were sawn in two, were
tempted, were slain with the sword. They wan-
dered about in sheepskins and goatskins, being
destitute, afflicted, tormented—of whom the
world was not worthy. They wandered in deserts
and mountains, in dens and caves of the earth.
*And all these, having obtained a good **testimony***
through faith, did not receive the promise, God
having provided something better for us, that
they should not be made perfect apart from us.

Hebrews states this reality in leading into the next statements concerning our being surrounded by these who obtained a good testimony of faith. This is speaking of their place of influence and authority in Heaven because of the lives they lived. The word "testimony" in the Greek is *martureo*. It means a judicial witness. When the Bible calls them the Great Cloud of Witnesses, it is on purpose. They literally have a judicial function in Heaven. They are not on a cloud playing a harp somewhere. They are still functioning to see the passion of God fulfilled on earth.

My own experience with the Great Cloud of Witnesses began many years ago, even though at the time I had no grid for it. This experience came through the venue of a dream. I thought it was a symbolic thing being shown me from the Lord. I now, however, believe it to have been a literal encounter with one from this spiritual dimension. I was not seeking out such an encounter; God, in His sovereignty, opened up this dimension and once more, this is the basis on which we are approaching this subject. We do not seek these encounters, but should God pull back the veil and grant us access, we need to know how to navigate such an experience.

We had moved into the healing anointing very strongly. We were seeing many healings and miracles occur. During the beginning stage of this ministry, I had this dream. Influential evangelist Smith Wigglesworth appeared to me and was sitting at breakfast with me. While the dream was going on and I was conversing with him, I was simultaneously thinking. I remember considering what was happening. I thought, *How can this be? I'm sitting here talking with Smith Wigglesworth. He's dead, but here I am talking to him.* I distinctly remember thinking that I wanted him to pray for me before I woke up. Even in the dream, I knew I was sleeping yet having this encounter. I, however, awoke before I could have him pray for me. Looking back on this encounter, I now know it wasn't symbolic. It was a literal experience with Smith Wigglesworth from the Great Cloud of Witnesses. I believe he had come to impart to me understanding of how to operate in the healing realm. This is why we were conversing in this setting.

There was an impartation being given me concerning walking in a similar realm that Smith Wigglesworth had walked in. The interesting thing to me is that I have always had this militant sphere I have operated in when praying for the sick. Psalm 92:10 speaks of this kind of anointing:

> *But my horn You have exalted like a wild ox; I have been anointed with fresh oil.*

I knew this was a realm that I gravitated to through the Holy Spirit's leading. I believe Smith Wigglesworth was allowed to impart to me understanding and even an anointing to function in this grace. This may sound crazy, but read on before any judgments are made against this idea.

Two Main Thoughts

In dealing with the Great Cloud of Witnesses and any contact we would have with them, there are two main thoughts. There are those who say we should never connect or interact with those who are already in Heaven. They say they are dead and therefore we are forbidden to have any interaction with them. There is even a term used to describe this—"necromancy" is defined as talking with the dead. Leviticus 20:6 is just one of several Scriptures where we are told not to have contact with the dead:

> *And the person who turns to mediums and familiar spirits, to prostitute himself with them, I will set My face against that person and cut him off from his people.*

A "medium" is one who supposedly can "call up" the spirits of people who had died. They are called mediums because they stand between the dead and the living and become connections between the two. The next part of this Scripture is very important, though. It speaks of *"familiar spirits."* The ones the mediums are speaking with are not really dead people. They are in fact communicating with spirits or demons that are familiar with the person desiring to be communicated with. They were probably assigned to this person during their time alive on the earth. Therefore, they know pertinent information about them. They can therefore masquerade as this person's spirit to deceive people into believing they are talking to the real spirit of the person.

This is what God declares several times in Scripture that we are not to involve ourselves in as His people. The punishment was very severe. God said He would set His face against these people and cut them off as part of His covenant people. If we or any of our ancestors have had anything to do with witchcraft, sorcery, fortune-telling, or speaking with mediums, we must repent. This actually is a very serious indictment. We need the blood of Jesus to cleanse us from this defilement and accusation against us.

When we read these kinds of Scriptures, it seems to make it unlawful for us to connect or interact with those who have died. Yet the Bible says these surround us. It appears that they are very close to us. This word "surround" in Hebrews 12:1 is the Greek word *perikeimai* and it means to lie around, to hang out, to enclose and encircle. They clearly are not on another planet or way up in Heaven somewhere disconnected from us. The idea is they are close and even joined to us. They are hanging out with us potentially. Heaven is not a distant place. Heaven is an atmosphere in the unseen realm. It is a spiritual dimension we transition into after our time on earth when we know the Lord and belong to Him. We will discuss this more in a later chapter.

So how do we deal with the fact that God said we were not to communicate with the dead or interact with them? The answer is found in two New Testament realities. The first one is that those who are born again are *not dead* even when they die naturally! Jesus was adamant about this. Matthew 22:31-32 makes a startling declaration. Jesus, in answering the Sadducees who did not believe in a resurrection from the dead, shows the power of God:

> *But concerning the resurrection of the dead, have you not read what was spoken to you by God, saying, "I am the God of Abraham, the God of Isaac, and the God of Jacob"?* **God is not the God of the dead, but of the living.**

The Lord, after Abraham, Isaac, and Jacob had physically died, declared He was their God. He was saying He was in a covenant relationship with them. Then He makes this statement, *"God is not the God of the dead but of the living."* Jesus is saying to these religious leaders, "You have it all wrong." Just because someone's physical body has ceased to operate doesn't mean the person is dead. The person is still very much alive.

This is true especially of those who belong to Jesus and are in covenant with God through Him. Even if the natural body ceases, the essence of who we are continues! We just transition into another realm of life. Jesus also addresses this truth when talking to Martha about Lazarus and his death. John 11:25-26 shows Jesus clearly declaring that we *never* die when we believe in Him:

> *Jesus said to her, "I am the resurrection and the life. He who believes in Me, though he may die, he shall live. And **whoever lives and believes in Me shall never die**. Do you believe this?"*

Jesus Himself states that when we believe in Him we *never* die. Our physical being may pass away temporarily, but we go on living. Biblically speaking, we are not dead. Those who would want to label us who believe in the Great Cloud of Witnesses and any encounters with them as involved in necromancy, don't understand this. They still see death from an Old Testament perspective.

When we enter a covenant with God through Jesus Christ, we pass from death to life! First John

3:14 proclaims we have left death and entered into life as His new creations:

> *We know that we have passed from death to life,*
> *because we love the brethren. He who does not*
> *love his brother abides in death.*

John says one of the signs that this has happened is our love for God's people. It is a signal that we no longer are in death but we have changed places in the spirit realm. We are now alive and cannot die. First Corinthians 15:53-57 defines for us the fact that death has no power over those who belong to Jesus:

> *For this corruptible must put on incorruption,*
> *and this mortal must put on immortality. So*
> *when this corruptible has put on incorrup-*
> *tion, and this mortal has put on immortality,*
> *then shall be brought to pass the saying that is*
> *written: "Death is swallowed up in victory. O*
> *Death, where is your sting? O Hades, where is*
> *your victory?" The sting of death is sin, and the*
> *strength of sin is the law. But thanks be to God,*
> *who gives us the victory through our Lord Jesus*
> *Christ.*

Paul is declaring that at the resurrection of the dead we will get new bodies. Our spirits that never die will have new bodies that are compatible with the life we have. We will have bodies that allow us to function fully in the life that never dies! Then death will fully be swallowed up in victory. It will no longer have any sting. Notice though that until that time our victory over death, hell, and the grave is through our Lord Jesus Christ. So not only those of us who are alive on earth that enjoy His life in us, but also those alive in Heaven have our victory in Jesus. We are all alive and death's sting and power has been broken. Hallelujah!

So the argument that we are speaking to the dead or being involved in necromancy is completely unbiblical. Those in the Great Cloud of Witnesses are alive.

The Purpose of God

There is one other fact I want to bring to your attention, however. The whole purpose of God is to bring Heaven and earth back together. Before the Fall in the Garden of Eden, there was no division of Heaven from earth. This is what made earth and Adam and Eve's existence paradise. When Adam and Eve rebelled and sinned, the division between Heaven and earth occurred. Ephesians 1:9-10 tells us the intent of God:

*Having made known to us the mystery of His will, according to His good pleasure which He purposed in Himself, that in the dispensation of the fullness of the times **He might gather together in one** all things in Christ, **both which are in heaven and which are on earth—in Him***.

God's intent through Jesus Christ is to again join Heaven and earth together. This is the mystery of His will and what He has purposed in Himself. When Jesus died on the Cross, the Bible says the veil was torn in two. Matthew 27:50-53 tells us about this:

And Jesus cried out again with a loud voice, and yielded up His spirit. Then, behold, the veil of the temple was torn in two from top to bottom; and the earth quaked, and the rocks were split, and the graves were opened; and many bodies of the saints who had fallen asleep were raised; and coming out of the graves after His resurrection, they went into the holy city and appeared to many.

The veil being torn in two was not just humankind now having access into the holiest of holies or God's awesome presence. That is of great importance, but it is not all that happened. When the veil tore, saints who had passed away in generations gone by were released from the bondage of death. They came out of their graves and appeared to many. They did this after Jesus' resurrection because He had to be the firstborn from the dead. Once He was resurrected, however, they came out of their now opened graves. Their appearing to many was in essence one of the first encounters with the Great Cloud of Witnesses.

This was because in the beginning stages of Heaven and earth being brought back together, the saints of old manifested to people still alive on earth. We have now for 2,000-plus years been in the process of Heaven and earth remerging together. This is why that before the climatic return of Jesus that will complete this merger, there will be increased encounters with the heavenly realm. God's passion to see Heaven and earth back together again will be fulfilled. That which stood in the way of Heaven and earth being joined together was removed as Jesus died on the Cross.

We now should have the expectation of encountering those from Heaven because Jesus' work on the Cross made it possible for Heaven and earth to be brought together once again. For those who are born again, they become alive to Christ (Romans 6:11). One expression of this is becoming alive to the spirit realm—the activity that the author of Hebrews says we have come to. As we keep our eyes fixed upon

Jesus, likewise, we need to be mindful of the activity taking place in the spiritual realm so we can live our Christian lives more effectively. The more we operate in agreement with the unseen realities of the Kingdom, the more we will see the Kingdom of God being demonstrated on earth.

When Adam and Eve fell from the place God had given them, all of creation was thrown into a fallen state. God's word to them was they would die should they ever disobey Him. Genesis 2:17 declares the consequences of their disobedient activities:

> *But of the tree of the knowledge of good and evil you shall not eat, for in **the day** that you eat of it you shall surely die.*

God told them they would die on *"the day"* they disobeyed. We know this did happen. They experienced separation from the closeness they had known with God. However, there was an ongoing dying that began. The life span of humans on earth became shorter and shorter. This separation caused the ability to hear God as the human race to get harder and harder. For instance, Cain even in his rebellion and killing of Abel was still able to carry on a conversation with God (Genesis 4:8-15). Today this would seem impossible.

Yet because this was so close to the time when the initial separation occurred, there was still an ability to talk to God and hear from Him. This is because the separation of Heaven and earth was a gradual one. In fact, the word God gave to Adam and Eve concerning them dying when they ate of the tree implied this. It literally says in the Hebrew, "dying you shall die." The consequence of their disobedience threw everything into a gradual but sure separation of Heaven from earth.

Just like the separation of Heaven and earth was progressive, the joining of Heaven and earth together again is also progressive. We have been being joined together with Heaven again for 2,000 years. Ever since Jesus' death, burial, resurrection, and ascension, Heaven and earth has been reuniting. Romans 5:18-19 tells us that Adam's sin propelled the earth into death. It also tells us that Jesus' obedience set in motion the recovering from that sin.

> *Therefore, as through one man's offense judgment came to all men, resulting in condemnation, even so through one Man's righteous act the free gift came to all men, resulting in justification of life. For as by one man's disobedience many were made sinners, so also by one Man's obedience many will be made righteous.*

The obedience of Jesus has recovered creation from its fallen state. We are progressively moving back into union with Heaven. The fullness of this will be seen at the second coming of Jesus Christ. There will then be a full manifestation of Heaven and earth being rejoined. First Corinthians 15:22-26 shows that Jesus is reigning through His church until all enemies are put under His feet.

> *For as in Adam all die, even so in Christ all shall be made alive. But each one in his own order: Christ the firstfruits, afterward those who are Christ's at His coming. Then comes the end, when He delivers the kingdom to God the Father, when He puts an end to all rule and all authority and power. For He must reign till He has put all enemies under His feet.* **The last enemy that will be destroyed is death**.

The last enemy that will be defeated is death at His coming. When Christ returns, there will then be the full manifestation of Heaven and earth being rejoined. Until this time, the merging of Heaven and earth continues. This can be why there is increased heavenly activity on earth. Revelation is increasing. Angels are manifesting. The Cloud of Witnesses is being seen and even interacting.

All this and much more are occurring because we are progressing toward the total union once again of God's heavenly and earthly creation. All of this testifies of the eternal power of the perfecting work of Jesus' blood. His perfect blood makes it possible for the reconciliation of God and humanity. Heaven and earth are functionally being joined together again! If anything, interaction with the Cloud of Witnesses testifies to the ultimate agenda of God: to bring Heaven and Earth back together.

The Scripture forbids us to communicate with the dead (Leviticus 20:6) and yet we see both Elijah and Moses on the Mount of Transfiguration (Matthew 17) speaking with Jesus in the company of three disciples who were witnesses to both the encounter and conversation. Both Elijah and Moses had departed for glory long ago but there they were.

The Scripture does not mention that Elijah died, rather he was taken up by a whirlwind into Heaven (2 Kings 2:11), but it is clear regarding the death of Moses. God Himself said, "Moses My servant is dead," meaning physical death (Joshua 1:2).

We know for sure that Jesus would not rebel against the Word and sin, as necromancy was punishable by death under the law. So what happened? Jesus declared, *"I am the resurrection and the life. He who believes in Me, though he may die, he shall live. And whoever lives and believes in Me shall never die. Do you believe this?"* (John 11:25-26).

I don't know about you, but I believe it! When you are in Christ, you have the gift of eternal life at the moment you believe and receive Him as your Savior. You aren't dead, you are very much alive whether your body still has breath in it while on earth or not. You become a member of God's household and His Kingdom from that moment on. Look at what the writer of Hebrews says in regard to this new life:

> *But you have come to Mount Zion and to the city of the living God, the heavenly Jerusalem, and to myriads of angels, to the general assembly and church of the firstborn who are enrolled in heaven, and to God, the Judge of all,* **and to the spirits of the righteous made perfect**, *and to Jesus, the mediator of a new covenant, and to the sprinkled blood, which speaks better than the blood of Abel* (Hebrews 12:22-24 New American Standard Bible).

We are *now* in His Kingdom, whether we live in a natural body in the earthly realm or have passed from this life into glory. If we have His life and His Kingdom within us, then we have access to the eternal dimensions of His being and Kingdom even while living in the earthly realm.

So then, what about Elijah and Moses? Jesus hadn't gone to the Cross yet when they passed. Were they saved? Did they have His life in them? The answer is *yes!* In the Old Testament, the faith of God's people was reckoned unto them as righteousness (James 2:23). That is why Jesus shared about Abraham's bosom (Luke 16:22). Abraham's bosom was a heavenly state beneath the earth where the righteous dead remained until Jesus finished His work on the Cross.

We know Moses was the law giver; and although the law is righteous, it cannot save us. So when did Moses come into salvation by grace? God revealed Christ to Moses in Exodus 33:19 when He said to him, *"I Myself will make all My goodness pass before you, and will proclaim the name of the Lord before you...."* The word "goodness" used in that verse is written in the superlative tense in the Hebrew. God was saying, I am going to reveal My maximum goodness to you (Christ), and I will proclaim His name to you! Jesus was revealed to Moses and Moses believed. That is why satan lost the battle over Moses' body as recorded in the book of Jude. Moses was saved through the revelation of Christ by faith. That is why he could speak with Jesus, Peter, James, and John—it wasn't necromancy because he wasn't dead!

When you know Jesus, you are not dead, you are very much alive—forever! In Christ, we are one Kingdom under God, and that begins the moment we are born again. We are on earth right now serving God's purposes; and those who have passed on before us are serving God in the eternal dimension, looking on at us.

Robert Henderson does an amazing job of powerfully explaining and unpacking this subject with various aspects and insights throughout this book, *The Great Cloud of Witnesses in the Courts of Heaven*.

I would never encourage a believer to intentionally seek out an encounter with someone who has gone on before us in the Great Cloud of Witnesses, as we are to seek Jesus. However, there could be times when God Himself wants you to see and connect into that realm.

My Encounter

The first time I had an encounter with those who were in the Great Cloud of Witnesses was around the year 2002 when I was in an airplane traveling to Europe on a ministry engagement. I was not looking for an encounter; in fact, I didn't even know at that time I could have an encounter with someone from the Great Cloud of Witnesses. As I was peacefully reading my Bible, three apostolic women in the spirit encircled me in the plane: Maria Woodworth-Etter, Aimee Semple McPherson, and Kathryn Kuhlman.

I am not going to go into the details of the encounter, but I will share the purpose of this experience. God revealed to me a number of years later that He sent them to pass on apostolic mantles for women and there would be an emergence of women apostles in our day. Since then God has used me to raise up and mentor many women into their callings. The commissioning for this mandate came through that encounter.

In sharing this experience, I know you may have questions and that is why you need to read Robert's book on this subject. It clarifies many things for you and offers answers to your questions. God is inviting us to experience a thin spot between the heavens and the earth and many believers are having similar encounters. As you read this book, may your spiritual eyes and understanding be open to behold and understand the truth revealed.

Oh Lord, may Your Kingdom come, Your will be done on earth as it is in Heaven. All for Your glory!

—Dr. Patricia King
Founder, Patricia King Ministries

Chapter 4

One Church in Heaven and Earth

WHEN we talk about the Great Cloud of Witnesses, we are speaking of the saints who are already in the heavenly realm. They are still an active part of the Church. Ephesians 3:14-15 reveals the way God sees us together:

For this reason I bow my knees to the Father of our Lord Jesus Christ, from whom the whole family in heaven and earth is named.

Apostle Paul said that those who are in Heaven and those who are on earth who belong to God are one family. We are one family because we have the same Father and carry His name. My wife, Mary, and all of our six children carry the name Henderson. This identifies us as being of the same family. The significance is that the father's name identifies the family and its DNA.

Paul was declaring that whether it's the portion of the family that is on earth or the portion of the family in Heaven, we all are of one Father. Because we are the same family and therefore His Church, whether in Heaven or earth, we are still striving for the same cause. We desire the Kingdom of God to be established on earth. We are still pressing for Heaven to come to earth!

Just because believers transition to Heaven doesn't mean they lose the passion of their lives. They still carry what they longed for while on earth. This is why Hebrews 11:39-40 tells us we are still very much connected with each other:

> *And all these, having obtained a good testimony through faith, did not receive the promise, God having provided something better for us, that they should not be made perfect apart from us.*

Notice that those who are in Heaven and we who are on earth receive our rewards together. We are so much still one people that we together will get what we labored for. God did not allow them to receive the fullness of the promise. He designed it in such a way that the generations of believers together will come into the fullness of the promises of the ages.

In other words, they need us and we need them. Even though they are in Heaven and we are on earth, we are still striving for the same prize. That prize is the manifestation of the Kingdom of God in fullness on earth. Revelation 11:15 tells us the whole world will once again be under the rulership of the Lord:

> *Then the seventh angel sounded: And there were loud voices in heaven, saying, "The kingdoms of this world have become the kingdoms of our Lord and of His Christ, and He shall reign forever and ever!"*

Those who are part of the Great Cloud of Witnesses are still passionate about their part of the kingdoms of the world becoming the Kingdoms of our Lord and His Christ. In other words, what their call was while on earth is still their passion and desire today while in Heaven. For instance, if they were called to Germany to see it become a nation reflecting God's glory, I believe this is still a functioning passion. This is the same concerning any region, state, city, or nation of the earth. The witnesses don't lose their passion because they transitioned to Heaven.

First Corinthians 13:12 could give us a little insight into this transition from earth to Heaven:

For now we see in a mirror, dimly, but then face to face. Now I know in part, but then I shall know just as I also am known.

Paul made this statement when speaking of the differences between living in the earthly realm and in the heavenly realm. What I presently know, the earthly realm will be greatly enhanced in the heavenly realm. It will not be diminished but increased. What I understand in the spiritual realm now will be even greater in the heavenly realm. This could mean the burden and passion of my heart on earth will even increase in the heavenly dimension because I am seeing face to face.

Those who are part of the Great Cloud of Witnesses don't change into different people just because they leave the earth realm. They simply change in their function from an earthly one to a heavenly one.

One of the central keys to seeing Heaven enter earth is Heaven and earth agreeing together. We see this in how Jesus said He performed miracles. In John 5:19 in response to the question of how the man at the pool of Bethesda was healed, Jesus says:

> *Most assuredly, I say to you, the Son can do*
> *nothing of Himself, but what He sees the Father*
> *do; for whatever He does, the Son also does in*
> *like manner.*

Jesus explained that whatever He saw happening
in Heaven, He then mimicked or did one earth. The
result was Heaven entering earth. Miracles came from
Heaven to earth because Heaven and earth came into
agreement. There is much activity in Heaven. In fact,
Hebrews 12:22-24 gives us at least some of that activity that we are to be part of or agree with:

> *But you have **come to** Mount Zion and to the*
> *city of the living God, the heavenly Jerusalem, to*
> *an innumerable company of angels, to the general*
> *assembly and church of the firstborn who are registered in heaven, to God the Judge of all, to the spirits of just men made perfect, to Jesus the Mediator*
> *of the new covenant, and to the blood of sprinkling*
> *that speaks better things than that of Abel.*

As mentioned previously, notice that we are told
we have *"come to"* all this activity in the spirit realm
or Heaven. We are in fact part of all this activity. One
of the things mentioned is *"the spirits of just men made
perfect."* This is a reference to the Great Cloud of
Witnesses. As New Testament believers, we are in the

same dimensions of the spirit world that they are. Our job is to agree with the present activity of Heaven so that it can come to earth. We do this by learning to live in two dimensions at the same time. Jesus spoke of this when talking to Nicodemus in John 3:13:

> *No one has ascended to heaven but He who came down from heaven, that is, the Son of Man who is in heaven.*

Jesus was talking to Nicodemus about being born again and the realm of Heaven it opens up. We have made being born again about going to Heaven when we die. Being born again is about awakening in the spirit to the heavenly realm right now. As we are told in John 17:3 by Jesus:

> *And this is eternal life, that they may know You, the only true God, and Jesus Christ whom You have sent.*

Being born again is experientially knowing God, and the way we do this is connecting to His Holy Spirit through our born-again spirit. Jesus was letting Nicodemus know that He as the Son of Man lived both in this earthly realm but also the heavenly realm as well. This is why Jesus could speak of *"doing what He saw the Father do."* This was a possibility because even though in the natural Jesus functioned on earth, in the spiritual realm, Jesus functioned from Heaven.

We also see Elijah referring to living in two realms in First Kings 17:1 when he is standing before King Ahab:

> *And Elijah the Tishbite, of the inhabitants of*
> *Gilead, said to Ahab, "As the Lord God of*
> *Israel lives, before whom I stand, there shall not*
> *be dew nor rain these years, except at my word."*

I used to think when Elijah spoke of standing before the Lord that he had been in a place of prayer, had heard God speak, and had come to proclaim it to Ahab. I now know that Elijah was practicing how Jesus said He lived, in two dimensions at one time. Elijah was declaring to Ahab that even though in the natural he was standing before him, in the spirit he was in the heavenly realm standing before the Lord. From this dimension of Heaven, Elijah was making a decree into the natural. He decreed it would not rain until he said it could.

Through this phenomenon, Heaven and earth came into agreement. This was because Elijah, like other prophets of those days, was living in two realms at one time! This is what we are called to as well. As born-again people, God would awaken us to the heavenly realm. In this heavenly realm we "have come to," there are the spirits of just men made perfect. As God's family on earth, we are to be agreeing with His family in Heaven. When we do, we pull Heaven to earth. The two are joined again and God's passion is fulfilled (see Ephesians 1:10).

Spirits Made Perfect

The phrase *"spirits of just men made perfect"* is worth examining. This is a reference to the place and status of those who are in the Great Cloud of Witnesses. First of all, they are spirit beings. Notice this is plural. The word "spirit" is the Greek word *pneuma*. It means a current of air or by analogy a spirit, a rational soul. We as believers understand this is who we are. As Kenneth Hagin would say, "We are a spirit, we have a soul, and we live in a body." First Thessalonians 5:23 shows our triune being:

> *Now may the God of peace Himself sanctify you*
> *completely; and may your whole **spirit, soul,***
> ***and body** be preserved blameless at the coming*
> *of our Lord Jesus Christ.*

In Heaven right now, prior to the resurrection from the dead, people are spirits who have a soul. They are waiting for the resurrection from the dead to have their perfect bodies. This could be some of what it means that they without us cannot be made perfect (see Hebrews 11:40). They need us to fulfill our portion of the plan of God for the ages so the culmination of history can occur. This would be the return of Jesus to the earth and the resurrection from the dead. At that time, the saints will have their glorified bodies. First Corinthians 15:50-54 tells us about the change that will occur to our bodies.

> *Now this I say, brethren, that flesh and blood cannot inherit the kingdom of God; nor does corruption inherit incorruption. Behold, I tell you a mystery: We shall not all sleep, but we shall all be changed—in a moment, in the twinkling of an eye, at the last trumpet. For the trumpet will sound, and the dead will be raised incorruptible, and we shall be changed. For this corruptible must put on incorruption, and this mortal must put on immortality. So when this corruptible has put on incorruption, and this mortal has put on immortality, then shall be brought to pass the saying that is written: "Death is swallowed up in victory."*

We shall go from corruption to incorruption and from mortal to immortal in a moment. We shall receive a new, resurrected body that can never die. This body will allow us to function both in the earthly realm and its atmosphere and in the heavenly realm and its atmo-sphere. We must receive this new body because our present one is not capable of inheriting the heavenly realm. This is why presently any encounter we have with Heaven must be from our spirits. Our bodies can-not function there until they are changed. Then we will have the capacity to even in our bodies live in the two realms unrestricted.

So the reason we have come to the *spirits* of just men made perfect is because they presently do not have their resurrected bodies. They are spirits in the heavenly realm. In that they are spirits plural, it means there are many of them. When the Bible calls them the *Great* Cloud of Witnesses, it is referring to the numbers and quantity of them. The word "great" is the Greek word *tosoutos* and it means so vast as this in regard to quantity, amount, numbers, much and many. In other words, it is speaking of the vast num-bers of them. There are so many of them that they are referred to as a cloud. One spirit of a person would not constitute a cloud. However, if there were hundreds, thousands, or even tens of thousands of spirits gath-ered together, it could result in a cloud.

The Glory Cloud

Years ago when I was pastoring in Texas, I looked up one morning and could not see the back wall of the sanctuary. This place could seat around 500 people, and there was a balcony that would hold additional people, but it wasn't normally used. There were probably 350 to 400 people present that day. I couldn't see the back wall and the back area of the sanctuary because what I thought was smoke had "rolled into" the sanctuary. It was the spring of the year in Texas.

As I was preaching, I became aware of this "smoke" and wondered where it came from. I remember thinking that the doors to the outside were open and smoke had drifted in from someone burning leaves. Suddenly, however, it dawned on me that I didn't smell smoke. This was when I realized the smoke must be spiritual.

I had heard about the "glory cloud," but had never seen it. There was a pretty strong move of God in the church at this time. People were being saved, healed, and delivered. The weight of God's presence had increased substantially. Now I was literally seeing smoke in the room. I remember calling the people's attention to it.

From this point on during our services, this smoke would appear frequently. At times it would look like smoke. At other times it was more like a cloud. There were even times when it was like a mist hanging in the air as the services progressed. I only knew to refer to it as the "glory cloud." I considered it to be the weight of God's presence tangibly manifesting.

I still believe this, but now I'm convinced something more was occurring. I believe it was a portion of the Great Cloud of Witnesses coming in. I had no concept for this then. I now, however, believe that what we consider the manifestation or expression of the glory of God can also contain spirits of just men made perfect. Even still, if the Cloud of Witnesses plays a role in this manifestation of glory, it's always to focus attention all the more on the reality, majesty and holiness of Jesus.

Cloud Encounters

To further substantiate this belief, I should tell you one more personal encounter. Yes, these are my own personal stories, however, I base these experiences on the Bible as well as my desire to encounter the supernatural of God. I am convinced we must have new levels of the supernatural without compromising the Word of God. If the level of supernatural we currently have could accomplish all that God requires, it would have been accomplished years ago. We must become settled in our theology so we can open ourselves to the supernatural without fear. We must know how to see Heaven and earth in agreement so Heaven can shake earth!

I had begun to have several encounters with the Cloud of Witnesses. This was happening through dreams, in church services, and other venues. I will share more of this as we progress. It seemed that this realm had opened to me. I am not saying it happened all the time, but frequently. I had, however, not really talked about it.

One Monday after Easter I was talking to my son, Adam, who pastors his own church. He began to tell me what happened during the Easter services he was leading the day before. He said that at the end of the services a cloud came into the sanctuary and the weight of God's presence intensified. He spoke of how special this was. Many of the people were aware of the Cloud and were swept up in the glory of God that came at the end of the service time.

We thanked God for that experience and how God was so faithful to honor the service and the people with His closeness. I simply stated, as Adam was telling this to me, that I had come to believe that "The Cloud" was more than just the presence of the Lord. I shared with him that I felt confident it was the Cloud of Witnesses who were being drawn to us and coming to be part of our gatherings. When I said this, Adam gasped and said, "Dad, I just remembered something that happened before the services as I was praying." He then told me that while he was praying before the services that morning, the Lord spoke to his spirit. He said he heard the Lord say that his Mamaw (his grandmother, my mother) would be in the services that day. That is not spectacular except for the fact that she had died several years before.

You must understand that this is not something we had ever talked about before. We hadn't talked against it, but definitely not for it either. For Adam to "hear" this was out of the ordinary at the very least. This is not something he would be given to or was gravitating toward. He was sure he had heard God say this. He, however, had not connected what God had said before the services to what happened at the end of the service time. When I spoke of the cloud being the Cloud of Witnesses, it triggered his remembrance.

I'm emphasizing this to say we didn't manufacture this situation. In fact, Adam didn't connect the dots until after the fact. Plus, I didn't know what God had said to him until after I spoke of the cloud of glory being the Cloud of Witnesses. I now believe that the smoke, cloud, and mist that would regularly hang in our services were in fact a constituency of the Cloud of Witnesses. This does have scriptural backing.

There are several places in the Bible where we see a cloud appearing. When Jesus was on the Mount of Transfiguration with His three disciples a cloud overshadowed them. Matthew 17:3-5 shows Moses, Elijah, and a cloud involved in this encounter:

> *And behold,* **Moses and Elijah appeared** *to*
> *them, talking with Him. Then Peter answered*
> *and said to Jesus, "Lord, it is good for us to be*
> *here; if You wish, let us make here three taber-*
> *nacles: one for You, one for Moses, and one for*
> *Elijah." While he was still speaking, behold,* **a**
> **bright cloud overshadowed them**; *and sud-*
> *denly* **a voice came out of the cloud**, *saying,*
> *"This is My beloved Son, in whom I am well*
> *pleased. Hear Him!"*

I think it's interesting that Moses and Elijah, who are definitely no longer alive in human bodies yet are clearly still alive, appear to Jesus. They are having a conversation. When Peter decides he needs to talk, a bright cloud overshadows them. By the way, this word "cloud" in both this Mount of Transfiguration encounter and Hebrews 12:1 is the same Greek word *nephos* and it means a cloud or cloudiness. There is no contradiction here. It could be that Moses and Elijah were not traveling alone. They were with a group of saints who overshadowed Peter and the other disciples. Moses and Elijah talked with Jesus, while the cloud of saints overshadowed the apostles. The word "overshadowed" in this Scripture passage is the Greek word *episkiazo* and means to cast a shade upon. It also means to envelop in a haze of brilliance and to invest with preternatural influence. This is the same word used in Luke 1:35 when the angel told Mary that the Holy Spirit would overshadow her:

> *And the angel answered and said to her, "The*
> *Holy Spirit will come upon you, and the power*
> *of the Highest will **overshadow** you; therefore,*
> *also, that Holy One who is to be born will be*
> *called the Son of God."*

The result of this "overshadowing" was an impregnation or impartation that occurred. Mary would begin to carry a holy child from the Lord who is our Lord Jesus Christ. Could it be that on the Mount of Transfiguration as the cloud overshadowed them, they received something from Heaven? If this was the Cloud of Witnesses, they were doing more than just hanging out. They were potentially participating in imparting and investing something into the emerging apostles. I will share more concerning this in a later chapter. Just suffice it to say here that it appears at times the Cloud of Witnesses has things to impart and invest into us in a spiritual dimension, as we are all connected as children of our heavenly Father.

Another place we see the cloud is when Jesus was taken up into Heaven after His resurrection. Acts 1:8-11 shows the cloud involved in Jesus' ascension:

> *But you shall receive power when the Holy Spirit*
> *has come upon you; and you shall be witnesses*
> *to Me in Jerusalem, and in all Judea and*
> *Samaria, and to the end of the earth. Now when*
> *He had spoken these things, while they watched,*
> *He was taken up, and **a cloud received Him***
> *out of their sight. And while they looked stead-*
> *fastly toward heaven as He went up, behold, two*
> *men stood by them in white apparel, who also*
> *said, "Men of Galilee, why do you stand gazing*
> *up into heaven? This same Jesus, who was taken*
> *up from you into heaven, will so come in like*
> *manner as you saw Him go into heaven."*

I don't believe the Bible states there was a cloud just to make us think it wasn't a clear day. There is a reason why a cloud received Him out of their sight. The word "receive" here is the Greek word *hupolam-bano* and it means to take from below, to carry upward. So the cloud was more than just moisture in the sky. It accompanied Him into Heaven. It could clearly be the Cloud of Witnesses welcoming Jesus back into Heaven after His complete obedience and faithful fulfillment of the Father's will on earth. I also think it is interesting the two "men" stood by the disciples and asked why they stood gazing up? The word "men" is the Greek word *aner*. It means a man, properly an individual male. Traditionally, many considered these two to be angels.

The Bible doesn't, however, call them angels. It says they were men. Could they have been from the Cloud of Witnesses? There are many instances in Scripture where, upon initial read and review, we assume we know exactly what the author is communicating. But in situations like this, we need to consider the possibility that perhaps there are more dimensions to what we are reading. Especially when we consider other portions in Scripture where the language is used.

For example, this cloud that accompanied Jesus will also be with Him when He returns again to earth. Matthew 24:30-31 reveals Jesus coming back in the clouds:

> *Then the sign of the Son of Man will appear in heaven, and then all the tribes of the earth will mourn, and they will see **the Son of Man coming on the clouds of heaven** with power and great glory. And He will send His angels with a great sound of a trumpet, and they will gather together His elect from the four winds, from one end of heaven to the other.*

Notice it's the *"clouds of heaven"* that Jesus comes back in. These are clouds from and assigned to the heavenly realm. We can get a little more idea concerning these clouds in Revelation 19:11-14. Here the Bible calls them the armies of Heaven:

> *Now I saw heaven opened, and behold, a white horse. And He who sat on him was called Faithful and True, and in righteousness He judges and makes war. His eyes were like a flame of fire, and on His head were many crowns. He had a name written that no one knew except Himself. He was clothed with a robe dipped in blood, and His name is called The Word of God. And the* **armies in heaven,** *clothed in fine linen, white and clean, followed Him on white horses.*

Clearly this is Jesus leading the armies of Heaven. Could this be the *"clouds of heaven"*? Everything is clothed in white and clean. The armies are even riding white horses. This could explain the appearance of this being as clouds in the sky at the coming of the Lord. The Great Cloud of Witnesses may be more prevalent in Scripture than we think. We will continue our examination of the spirit of just men made perfect in the next chapter.

Oh Happy Day

The Lord has gone to great lengths to help me understand and embrace the Great Clouds of Witnesses. Several years ago, I was preparing to teach on this subject, as I understood it then. I had told no one about my thoughts and ideas at this time. I was concerned that they wouldn't be received. I, in fact, hadn't even told any of it to my wife, Mary, at this time. I thought it could sound so weird that even she would reject it. One night I went to bed with the intent to arise and put together the message I would teach the next evening.

When I awoke the next morning, Mary greeted me with the words, "I had a dream last night." She proceeded to tell me her dream. My dad, who had died 15-plus years before, had come to her during the night in her dream. He began to tell her he had not liked the funeral we had for him years before. He wanted another funeral. This time he wanted an African children's choir to sing "Oh Happy Day." He told her that since he had "died," he had seen one singing this and wanted it for his "new funeral."

This was amazing to me. My wife had no awareness that I was about to tell her about my revelation concerning the Cloud of Witnesses, and here she was telling me about her encounter the night before. This spoke volumes to me and was somewhat confirming to say the least. The result, I put my message together and we also found the best version we could of an African children's choir singing "Oh Happy Day." That night I taught and told the story of my wife's dream.

At the end of the teaching, we played the song in honor of my dad and his request. I spoke of how I would not be who I am if it hadn't been for him and his hunger for God. As we did this, the presence of God came, but I also believe the glory of the Cloud of Witnesses showed up as well. To this day, I believe God allowed this so I could continue my journey to discovering this dimension of the spirit. We have much to learn yet.

Chapter 5

Just and Perfected

WE are told in Hebrews 12:23 that we have come to the *"spirits of just men made perfect."* Again, this is a reference to the Cloud of Witnesses. What does it mean when the Bible says this Cloud of Witnesses is made up of just men made perfect? The word "just" is the Greek word *dikaios* and it means to be equitable in character or act. By implication it means to be innocent and holy. To be equitable means to be fair and impartial. It means to be unbiased and unprejudiced. So to be just means be able to render good decisions without partiality or bias.

This definition kind of sounds like something legal is involved here and maybe even something a judge would do. This would make sense because we are talking about the Great Cloud of *Witnesses.* The word "witness" is the Greek word *martus* and it means a witness judicially. So, the Great Cloud of Witnesses is made up of just people who can render unbiased and impartial decisions. They can give unprejudiced testimonies in the Courts of Heaven.

If you happen to be reading this and have not read any of my other books on the Courts of Heaven, or are unfamiliar with this idea, let me briefly explain. When Jesus taught on prayer in the book of Luke, He addresses prayer from three distinct ideas. In His effort to unveil concepts governing prayer to His disciples, He placed prayer as approaching God as Father, Friend, and Judge. In Luke 11:2, Jesus tells the disciples that God is their Father:

> *So He said to them, "When you pray, say: Our Father in heaven, hallowed be Your name. Your kingdom come. Your will be done on earth as it is in heaven."*

Most will recognize this as what is traditionally called the "Lord's Prayer." However, Jesus was instructing the disciples that God was their Father and we should by faith approach Him in this manner. Jesus continued, telling them about God being their Friend. Luke 11:5 says that by faith we are to see God as our Friend and approach Him in this manner:

> *And He said to them, "Which of you shall have*
> *a friend, and go to him at midnight and say to*
> *him, 'Friend, lend me three loaves.'"*

If we were to go deeper in these realms of prayer, we would discover that approaching God as Father is about our needs. We would further discover that approaching God as Friend is about the needs of others. All of this is explained in my other books dealing with prayer and the Courts of Heaven.

Jesus placed prayer in a third dimension as well. He said in prayer we should also approach God as the Judge. This is found in Luke 18:1-8:

> *Then He spoke a parable to them, that men*
> *always ought to pray and not lose heart, saying:*
> *"There was in a certain city a judge who did*
> *not fear God nor regard man. Now there was a*
> *widow in that city; and she came to him, saying,*
> *'Get justice for me from my adversary.' And*
> *he would not for a while; but afterward he said*
> *within himself, 'Though I do not fear God nor*
> *regard man, yet because this widow troubles me*
> *I will avenge her, lest by her continual coming*
> *she weary me.'" Then the Lord said, "Hear*
> *what the unjust judge said. And shall God not*
> *avenge His own elect who cry out day and night*
> *to Him, though He bears long with them? I tell*

you that He will avenge them speedily. Never-
theless, when the Son of Man comes, will He
really find faith on the earth?"

In this parable Jesus is not saying God is an unrighteous judge we must convince. His point is that if this widow can secure a verdict on her behalf from this unrighteous judge, then how much more can we have our petitions granted from God as the righteous Judge of all the earth. We must recognize, however, that God as Judge rules over a judicial system called the Courts of Heaven. Daniel 7:10 gives us a glimpse into this judicial place of the spirit:

A fiery stream issued and came forth from before
Him. A thousand thousands ministered to Him;
ten thousand times ten thousand stood before
Him. The court was seated, and the books were
opened.

As God sits on His throne with thousands upon thousands worshipping and ministering to Him, there is a realm of spiritual operation where the Judge of all the earth oversees a Court. This is the dimension of the spirit where we by faith can enter and function. This is why Jesus in the third realm of prayer placed it in a judicial system before a judge. The Great Cloud of Witnesses as just men made perfect are part of this judicial order! They provide a needed and essential function as the Cloud of Witnesses in this heavenly realm. As a result of the formation of their character while on earth, they are trusted witnesses in Heaven's Court.

To really get this, we should examine a few more Scriptures. As previously cited, Hebrews 11:37-40 shows us the place these witnesses have been given as a result of their sacrifice on earth:

> *They were stoned, they were sawn in two, were tempted, were slain with the sword. They wandered about in sheepskins and goatskins, being destitute, afflicted, tormented—of whom the world was not worthy. They wandered in deserts and mountains, in dens and caves of the earth. And all these, having obtained a good* **testimony** *through faith, did not receive the promise, God having provided something better for us, that they should not be made perfect apart from us.*

Notice as a result of their sacrifice for the purposes of God on earth these have obtained a *"good testimony."* Again, the word "testimony" is the Greek word *martureo*. It means a witness, to testify and give evidence. When it says they have obtained a good testimony, it is speaking of their status in the spirit world. They carry a weight of authority because of their proven character of being just! From what I can see in Scripture, the good testimony is something that we need to be effective in the Courts of Heaven— whether we are living in the earthly realm or heavenly realm. The more good testimony we have, the more influence we have in the Courts of Heaven. As a side note here, we are saved completely by the grace of God. This is not a salvation conversation; this is a matter of both rewards in eternity and having Kingdom influence in the here and now. It's not how much earthly fame or recognition one has that gains such influence; it's faithfulness to the assignment of God on his or her life. Also, this is not a call to sinless perfectionism; it's a reminder to faithfully steward the life you've been entrusted with, giving Jesus your everything.

Those who are part of the Great Cloud of Witnesses have tremendous authority and influence because of the lives they lived. We should realize that all those mentioned in Hebrews 11, which many call the "hall of fame of faith" chapter, are in the Cloud of Witnesses. They walked in faith and made tremendous sacrifices for the Kingdom of God. They gave their lives so that the Kingdom of God would advance. It bears remembering that the word "witness" in Scripture is where we get the word "martyr." Remember that in Acts 1:8 Jesus uses this word "witness" to describe what the disciples and apostles would be and do:

> *But you shall receive power when the Holy Spirit has come upon you; and you shall be* **witnesses** *to Me in Jerusalem, and in all Judea and Samaria, and to the end of the earth.*

Jesus said they would be *"witnesses to Me."* This is the Greek word *martueo* and it means one who gives judicial testimony, but also one who is a martyr. The first apostles of the Lamb died martyr's deaths, except John. They gave their natural lives for the purpose of the gospel and the advancement of the Kingdom of God. However, we don't have to die naturally for this cause to obtain the good testimony that gives us status in the Courts of Heaven. We do, however, have to be willing to lay down our soulish lives or own desires at times, for God's purposes. Whoever gives up their life to fulfill God's will, will obtain for themselves a good testimony. This is what Revelation 12:10-11 tells us about successfully operating in the Courts of Heaven:

> *Then I heard a loud voice saying in heaven, "Now salvation, and strength, and the kingdom of our God, and the power of His Christ have come, for the accuser of our brethren, who accused them before our God day and night,*

The Cloud of Witnesses in the Courts of Heaven

> *has been cast down. And they overcame him by*
> *the blood of the Lamb and by the word of their*
> *testimony, and they did not love their lives to the*
> *death.*

The word "accuser" mentioned here is the Greek word *kategoros*. It means to be against someone in the assembly, a complainant at law. In other words, this is a judicial setting where an accusation is being made against us. The Bible is clear that we overcome these accusations and the accuser by the blood of the Lamb, the word of our testimony, and not loving our lives unto death. We undo any case against us by the blood of the Lamb. We present our own case in the Courts of Heaven through the word of our testimony, and we have a good testimony that lets us be heard and have influence because we have loved not our lives even unto death. We have been willing to lay our lives down for God's purposes.

Heavenly Realm of Influence

Those who are part of the Great Cloud of Witnesses were willing to operate in this dimension. They may not have actually died a martyr's death, but they forsook their own desires and gave themselves to the passion of the Lord. This has positioned them in heavenly realms with influence from the Great Cloud of Witnesses.

As I look at Scripture, I'm not sure that everyone who is born again actually is part of the Great Cloud of Witnesses. I hear talk about people who have died and that they are now in this Cloud. However, it seems to me that this part of Heaven is reserved for those who lived uniquely sacrificial lives in obedience to the Lord's will. All who have put their confidence and faith in the Lord Jesus Christ shall be saved (Romans 10:9). However, they may not all have a place as a part of this Cloud of Witnesses. Paul even wrote that there would be those who would be saved but *"so as through fire."* First Corinthians 3:14-15 tells us that each person's work done in this life will be tested in regard to eternal rewards and placement in Heaven:

> *If anyone's work which he has built on it endures, he will receive a reward. If anyone's work is burned, he will suffer loss; but he himself will be saved, yet so as through fire.*

If this is true, then our position in Heaven will be predicated on the way we lived our lives on earth. Salvation is not all about works—though it is important (James 2:17,26)—we must be faithful to the assignment and calling the Lord has entrusted to us. Jesus even spoke of the need to live a life where we willingly sacrifice our desires for His Kingdom. Matthew 10:38-39 tells us if we surrender our lives we will indeed find life:

> *And he who does not take his cross and follow after Me is not worthy of Me. He who finds his life will lose it, and he who loses his life for My sake will find it.*

When Jesus speaks of taking up our cross, it is a symbolic statement of forsaking our own passions to come after Him fully. This obviously doesn't mean we literally die on a cross as He did. It does, however, mean that through the power of His Spirit and grace we are willing to order our life away from our natural passions and into His desire for us. The word "life" in the Greek is *psuche*. It refers to what we would normally call the soul. The idea here is that we are willing to lay down anything that would conflict with what the Lord would require of us in obedience.

From what I can see in Scripture, everyone who obtains to the Cloud of Witnesses are those who lived this kind of life on earth. Their passion became to fulfill the Lord's will at all cost! The more we allow this spirit to be in us, the more we will qualify to function in the Cloud of Witnesses ourselves as our time of departure approaches.

As we read through Hebrews chapter 11 and see all those mentioned who lived these kinds of lives, it becomes clear they were obedient to their heavenly call. There is very powerful statement in Hebrews 11:32-35. The writer of Hebrews mentions people we know from Scripture, as well as others who are unknown. They were simply people who fulfilled their assignment from God and obtained for themselves a great place in the heavenly realm:

> *And what more shall I say? For the time would fail me to tell of Gideon and Barak and Samson and Jephthah, also of David and Samuel and the prophets: who through faith subdued kingdoms, worked righteousness, obtained promises, stopped the mouths of lions, quenched the violence of fire, escaped the edge of the sword, out of weakness were made strong, became valiant in battle, turned to flight the armies of the aliens. Women received their dead raised to life again. Others were tortured, not accepting deliverance, that they might obtain a better resurrection.*

Wow! There were those who could have been delivered from the hardships their obedience caused them, but they chose not to accept it. This was because they had a great awareness and respect for the position it was granting them in the heavenly realm. They are now enjoying and functioning from this place eternally because of the temporary choice to endure. It is clear that as we lay down our lives and love them not unto death we obtain for ourselves a far more *"eternal weight of glory"* (2 Corinthians 4:17).

Heavenly Court Proceeding

There is a young man I know in another country who had an experience with someone from the Cloud of Witnesses. This young man had been in a very severe car accident. Everyone concerned with the situation said it was a miracle he was still alive. His stay in the hospital was for an extended period of time. During his time in the hospital, he was in a coma. They did not know at this point whether he would live or die. The young man did, in fact pull through and live.

After he came out of the coma, he shared what had happened to him. While in the coma he found himself in Heaven. There was a Court proceeding in Heaven being held concerning him. The case being considered in this Court was whether this young man should die and simply come to Heaven or should he be allowed to live and fulfill his destiny on earth. He watched as this case concerning him proceeded. He said there were several witnesses and voices in the Court speaking from both perspectives. Some were advocating that he should simply come on to Heaven. There were other voices, however, saying that he should stay on earth and fulfill his destiny.

As he watched and the Court proceeding continued, he saw an older man with a long, white beard enter the Court. This man began to advocate before the Court that the young man should stay on earth and fulfill his destiny. This man had such great authority in this realm that the Court reached its verdict on the basis of this one testimony. The young man would be allowed to finish his destiny and live out his days on the earth. This, in fact, has happened. The young man is fully restored and fulfilling his destiny. Let me, though, finish this story.

As the young man watched this play out from his comatose state in the natural, but very real viewpoint in the spirit, the older man turned to leave the Court after the verdict was rendered. As he was leaving, the young man called to this witness who had helped secure his destiny. He said he called, "Sir, Sir." He said the man kept walking. The young man called again, "Sir." The witness kept walking without responding. The young man said he called the third time, "Sir." And this time the man stopped and looked at him. He then asked the man who had given the testimony, "Sir, what is your name?" The man responded, "My name is Noah" as he turned and exited the courtroom.

What a phenomenal story. If you believe this as I do, this man had Noah stand on his behalf to secure his destiny on earth. Noah's testimony came into agreement with the plan and purpose of God for this young man, and as a result, this intercessory agreement in Heaven granted him the ability to fulfill his destiny.

How amazing. Yet this lines up with the scriptural fact that these witnesses in Heaven are testifying in the Courts of Heaven. They, because of their obedience and surrender to the Lord, have been granted a good testimony or status in Heaven that allows their words to carry great impact. It appears that those who are in the Cloud of Witnesses function in this area of the Courts of Heaven. Another Scripture worth examining is Ezekiel 14:13-14. These verses show God pinpointing Noah, Daniel, and Job:

> *"Son of man, when a land sins against Me by persistent unfaithfulness, I will stretch out My hand against it; I will cut off its supply of bread, send famine on it, and cut off man and beast from it. Even if these three men, Noah, Daniel, and Job, were in it, they would deliver only themselves by their righteousness," says the Lord God.*

These three men clearly carried great weight before Heaven. At the time Ezekiel is prophesying this, Noah and Job have already died. Daniel, on the other hand, was a contemporary of Ezekiel. So God is saying even if those in Heaven agreed with those on earth—judgment could not be averted. The sin of the land is too much. Noah and Job were already in Heaven while Daniel was yet on earth.

The point I am making is that all of these men are still recognized by Heaven and are still functioning. Their righteousness has obtained for themselves a great place before the Lord and His Courts. This means we can function in the Courts of Heaven while yet on the earth. We can be esteemed by Heaven even as those who are already standing in place as witnesses of the Lord.

To finish these ideas in the chapter, notice that these are just men made perfect, which speaks that while on earth they were considered "just" or "justified." Romans 5:1 says that we are justified by faith:

> *Therefore, having been justified by faith, we have peace with God through our Lord Jesus Christ.*

The word "justified" in the Greek is the word *dikaioo* and it means to render just or innocent. So when the Bible says they are *"just men made perfect,"* it is declaring that in this life on earth, they were considered just because of their faith. Remember, *"the just shall live by faith."* This is what Romans 1:17 proclaims:

> *For in it the righteousness of God is revealed from faith to faith; as it is written,* **"The just shall live by faith."**

We obtain the righteousness and justness of the Lord when we by faith yield to the Lord and obey Him. This allows us to be considered "just" by the standards of Heaven. This is what those who are in the Cloud of Witnesses have done. Their faith and obedience toward God and His Son Jesus have granted them a standing in Heaven before they get there. Once they are there, they become "perfect." The imperfections of the flesh are removed and they are liberated to serve God without these. I believe this is the perfection that is spoken of. They no longer have the battles associated with the flesh and its temptations. Therefore, they are now the spirit of just men made perfect.

One other thought concerning this. Hebrews 12:23 makes this statement concerning the spirit of just men made perfect. However, in referring to these in the Cloud of Witnesses, Hebrews 11:40 says they cannot be made perfect without us:

*God having provided something better for us, that
they should not be made perfect apart from us.*

In reference to this Great Cloud of Witnesses,
one place declares them imperfect and in need of our
involvement. The other place says they are perfect. I
understand that in their present position in Heaven,
they are perfect in spirit and soul. They no longer have
the struggles of the flesh to wrestle with. However,
only when the coming generations of believers fulfill
their mandate from the Lord can the *"end of all things"*
occur (1 Peter 4:7). In other words, when we in agreement with Heaven and see all other enemies put under
Jesus' footstool, only then will Jesus return. Hebrews
10:13 declares Jesus is waiting for this to happen:

*From that time waiting till His enemies are made
His footstool.*

The Church of God's people must accomplish
the remaining purposes of God on earth. When this
happens, not only will those in Heaven be perfect in
spirit and soul, but they will receive their immortal
bodies as well. Philippians 3:20-21 tells us of this miracle that will occur:

*For our citizenship is in heaven, from which we
also eagerly wait for the Savior, the Lord Jesus*

> *Christ, who will **transform our lowly body**
> *that it may be conformed **to His glorious body**,*
> *according to the working by which He is able*
> *even to subdue all things to Himself.*

All who belong to the Lord in Heaven and on earth will experience this change. They will receive a glorious body. This body will be like the body Jesus came out of the grave with. We know this is correct because First Thessalonians 4:15-18 says the bodies of the saints who have died will rise first:

> *For this we say to you by the word of the Lord,*
> *that we who are alive and remain until the*
> *coming of the Lord will by no means precede*
> *those who are asleep. For the Lord Himself will*
> *descend from heaven with a shout, with the voice*
> *of an archangel, and with the trumpet of God.*
> *And the dead in Christ will rise first. Then we*
> *who are alive and remain shall be caught up*
> *together with them in the clouds to meet the Lord*
> *in the air. And thus we shall always be with the*
> *Lord. Therefore comfort one another with these*
> *words.*

At this point the Great Cloud of Witnesses will be perfected. All of us together will be rejoined to the Lord. Those in Heaven and those on earth will meet Him in the air. This will be a reunification of the Church on earth and the Church in Heaven. All of us shall then be perfect in spirit, soul, and body—forever to be with the Lord.

Up until this glorious day, which does hinge on those of us yet on earth obediently fulfilling God's will, we must function with the Church on earth and the Church in Heaven. As we learn to move in harmony and agreement, we can see a manifestation of Heaven on earth. We will see Jesus' Kingdom established.

In the next chapters, we will learn more about how to interact, cooperate, and move in agreement with the Church in Heaven, the Great Cloud of Witnessess.

One day, I was pulled up to Heaven and I experienced the Cloud of Witnesses myself. I was drawn to and intrigued by the enormous amount of people in the room. They were dressed in white robes and carried a peace about them. Their mannerisms were a bit alarming to me at first. The peace, joy, and honest love they carried felt amazing—and showed me my own lack.

Although they carried such peace, they weren't there to make peace; they were there to make war!

Prayers, intercession, and declarations were made loudly throughout the room. Not one by one, but rather all at once. It sounded like a war cry. It sounded like thunder shattering the air. That's when I decided I wanted to join in!

Prior to this experience, I had mistakenly always pictured the Cloud of Witnesses in a more passive role. I imagined them sitting in Heaven, looking down on us here on earth with love.

But they are anything but passive!

What will we do in Heaven, you might ask? I am convinced that not only do we passionately fall in love and worship our King Jesus who is worthy of all our adoration, but we also have jobs and roles in Heaven.

Walking into that room and hearing the prophetic decrees and cries from the Great Cloud of Witnesses made me hunger to match my prayers to theirs. How incredible would it be if you could pray what's on Heaven's heart? What's on the heart of the Father today? Those are the prayers I want to be praying and releasing.

John 5:19 says, *"Most assuredly, I say to you, the Son can do nothing of Himself, but what He sees the Father do...."*

At some point, we have to rise up to the position where we can step beyond the veil of just what we see in the natural and pray from the Father's perspective. The earth is crying out for the outpouring of the Spirit; and as we press in for revival, I believe it is key that we match the Father's heartbeat.

—Ana Werner
Author of *The Seer's Path* and *Seeing Behind the Veil*
Ana Werner Ministries
anawerner.org

Chapter 6

Reunifying Heaven and Earth

WE have seen that according to Ephesians 1:10 that it is the Lord's passion to join Heaven and earth together again:

> *That in the dispensation of the fullness of the times **He might gather together in one** all things in Christ, both which are in heaven and which are on earth—in Him.*

The closer we get to the fullness of the times as is mentioned here, the more Heaven and earth are being gathered together. So often we look for something to happen all at once. However, as the Kingdom of God has been expanding for 2,000-plus years, everything has been pressing together back into God's harmony. Instead of just one climatic event to push everything back together that was separated at the Fall, a series of progressive things occur that moves things together.

This is one of the reasons why more and more people are having encounters with Heaven. This is why the prophetic is becoming more abounding. This is why new terms are arising in churches to describe those who are encountering Heaven and its powers. Terms such as mystics, extreme prophetic, even Courts of Heaven and others are efforts to describe some of what is happening. The activities of Heaven and the activities of earth are merging. We must have new dimensions of the supernatural to see the fullness of God's purposes manifest. Part of this involves working with the Great Cloud of Witnesses and the encounters this brings.

We have seen in earlier chapters where people had encounters with these witnesses from Heaven. Let me reiterate that this is a "legal" occurrence. In other words, we are not doing something outside of spiritual boundaries that would be wrong. Hebrews 12:22-24 again tells us "where" we have come to in the spirit world!

> But **you have come to** Mount Zion and to the
> city of the living God, the heavenly Jerusalem,
> to an innumerable company of angels, to the
> general assembly and church of the firstborn who

are registered in heaven, to God the Judge of all,
to the spirits of just men made perfect, to Jesus
the Mediator of the new covenant, and to the
blood of sprinkling that speaks better things than
that of Abel.

In that we have *"come to"* all this activity, it means that we are seated in it and are part of it in the heavenly realm. Even though we are in the earthly dimension, we are also part of this heavenly realm we have come to. This means that prophetically we should not just hear an occasional word from God. We should also have encounters with all this activity we are in the midst of. We can see angels, hear words from Heaven, encounter the Judge, witness the blood speaking, agree with Jesus as our Mediator, and many other things. According to the subject of this book, we are to also encounter the spirits of just men made perfect. Our prophetic realms should increase to participate with Heaven and the Cloud of Witnesses.

If we are to interact with the Great Cloud of Witnesses in the Courts of Heaven, there are some guidelines we should follow. Let me again irrevocably proclaim that I advocate being open to such encounters and interactions. I see these in Scripture and believe they are valid for us today. We not only should desire these, we need them to see God's will completed on earth. Having clearly said this, we should, however, make sure we follow proper proto-col. Otherwise we can get into treacherous spiritual territory that can harm any and all involved. There are evil and demonic spirits who would masquerade as those from the Great Cloud of Witnesses. They would like nothing better than to deceive the saints of God. We must use proper behavior in functioning in these realms. I provide such things I feel are imperative to safely traversing these realms of the spirit.

Safeguards

The first and most important is to be open to these encounters and visitations and **make Jesus your pursuit.** Do not make the encounters what you are after. The writer of Hebrews in talking about the Great Cloud of Witnesses said that even though they are in the same spiritual dimension we are in, we must look to Jesus. Hebrews 12:1-2 tells us this very important safeguard:

> *Therefore we also, since we are surrounded
> by so great a cloud of witnesses, let us lay
> aside every weight, and the sin which so easily
> ensnares us, and let us run with endurance the
> race that is set before us, **looking unto Jesus,**
> the author and finisher of our faith, who for the
> joy that was set before Him endured the cross,*

despising the shame, and has sat down at the
right hand of the throne of God.

Notice that we are to be *"looking unto Jesus"* and not the activity of the spirit realm we are in. When Jesus and our love for Him is our compelling force, we will not go very far off. We must make Jesus our goal, our aim, and our target. If in the pursuit of Him we encounter other spiritual things, then this is fine. If, however, we make the encounters our purpose, we can get dangerously close to being deceived. Jesus must always be the main focus.

The Bible says that Jesus is the door. John 10:9 shows Jesus proclaiming Himself to be the door:

I am the door. If anyone enters by Me, he will be
saved, and will go in and out and find pasture.

Jesus is the door to our salvation. He is, however, also the door into the realms of the spirit. We must always enter the spirit realms through Him and our intimacy and faith in Him. There are other ways into the spirit realm. Witchcraft, drug use, sorcery, and intended and unintended cooperation with demons can bring people into the spirit realm. We must be very careful to only enter the realm of the spirit through our door—Jesus. He must be our pursuit. In my estimation, this is the downfall of Saul, the first king of Israel. He, in desperation, went to a witch and had her call up Samuel so he could talk to him. This is found in First Samuel 28:11-16:

> Then the woman said, "Whom shall I bring up for you?"
>
> And he [Saul] said, "Bring up Samuel for me."
>
> When the woman saw Samuel, she cried out with a loud voice. And the woman spoke to Saul, saying, "Why have you deceived me? For you are Saul!"
>
> And the king said to her, "Do not be afraid. What did you see?"
>
> And the woman said to Saul, "I saw a spirit ascending out of the earth."
>
> So he said to her, "What is his form?"
>
> And she said, "An old man is coming up, and he is covered with a mantle." And Saul perceived that it was Samuel, and he stooped with his face to the ground and bowed down.
>
> Now Samuel said to Saul, "Why have you disturbed me by bringing me up?"
>
> And Saul answered, "I am deeply distressed; for the Philistines make war against me, and God has departed from me and does not answer me

anymore, neither by prophets nor by dreams.
Therefore I have called you, that you may reveal
to me what I should do."

Then Samuel said: "So why do you ask me,
seeing the Lord has departed from you and has
become your enemy?

Some have said this wasn't really Samuel. I believe
that it was. There are several reasons for this. First,
what he told Saul did occur. Saul did die in battle.
Another reason why this was the real Samuel is God
didn't judge Saul for talking to Samuel. He judged
him for the "door" he went through. First Chronicles
10:13-14 says Saul died not because of speaking to
Samuel, but for going through the door of a familiar
spirit:

So Saul died for his unfaithfulness which he had
committed against the Lord, because he did not
keep the word of the Lord, and also because he
consulted a medium for guidance. But he did
not inquire of the Lord; therefore He killed him,
and turned the kingdom over to David the son of
Jesse.

Saul entered the spirit realm through the use of
a medium. This was forbidden. Anyone who uses
these means to access the spiritual dimension can be

releasing deadly forces against themselves and their houses. Even though Saul accessed this realm illegally, he still encountered the real Samuel.

The third clue that this was really Samuel is the medium was shocked when the real Samuel showed up. She was used to deceiving spirits masquerading as human spirits. She knew instantly that this was the real deal. It shocked her and made her afraid. My reason for pointing this out is that we must only go through Jesus as our door into the spiritual and heavenly realm. He is the only legal and safe conduit through which we can access these dimensions. We must always be looking unto Jesus, the Author and Finisher of our faith.

Another key to encountering the Cloud of Witnesses is to develop and grow in our prophetic sensitivity. Hebrews 5:14 tells us that by reason of use these abilities develop:

> But solid food belongs to those who are of full age, that is, those who by **reason of use** have their senses exercised to discern both good and evil.

The more we endeavor to function in the unseen realm, the more proficient we become at it. There are those who are highly gifted in these areas. I notice that so many of them that carry weighty gifting have witchcraft in their bloodline. Many times they themselves have past experiences in sorcery as well. These folks have to sanctify the gifting they have received by inheritance in the spirit realm. Otherwise the demon powers will try and interfere. The gift they have will not operate with purity. Once, however, the bloodline is cleansed, these gifts can be powerful through them for the Kingdom of God.

Even if we have no history of these prophetic giftings, they can be developed. I personally believe all of God's people have the potential to be prophetic. They need to just realize it and start to use it. For instance, when Jesus spoke of His ability to see prophetically in John 5:19-20, He said it was because the Father loved Him, not because of a gift:

> *Then Jesus answered and said to them, "Most assuredly, I say to you, the Son can do nothing of Himself, but what He sees the Father do; for whatever He does, the Son also does in like manner. For the Father loves the Son, and shows Him all things that He Himself does; and He will show Him greater works than these, that you may marvel."*

This is amazing to me. I don't need a gift to see from. I need instead to develop intimacy with God as my Father. When I do, the prophetic realm of seeing can open and I can perceive into the spirit. The more I walk with the Father in this intimate place, the more I can, through reason of use, exercise my spiritual senses to discern the activity in the spirit. Everyone must simply believe they have the ability by virtue of the born-again experience. If they will do this, they will be surprised and amazed at the realms that become available to them.

This is what Jesus sought to communicate to Nicodemus about being born again. In John 3:7-13 we see Jesus seeking to educate Nicodemus concerning these places in the spirit:

> *"Do not marvel that I said to you, 'You must be born again.' The wind blows where it wishes, and you hear the sound of it, but cannot tell where it comes from and where it goes. So is everyone who is born of the Spirit."*
>
> *Nicodemus answered and said to Him, "How can these things be?"*
>
> *Jesus answered and said to him, "Are you the teacher of Israel, and do not know these things? Most assuredly, I say to you, We speak what We know and testify what We have seen, and you do not receive Our witness. If I have told you earthly things and you do not believe, how will*

*you believe if I tell you heavenly things? No one
has ascended to heaven but He who came down
from heaven, that is, the Son of Man who is in
heaven."*

Jesus wanted Nicodemus to know that when born
again, he would have the capacity to live in both the
natural and the spiritual realms at the same time. We
haven't been taught what the born-again experience
grants us. We think we simply get to go to Heaven.
Jesus actually said we could have heavenly encounters now! This is what He meant when He said as
the One who came down from Heaven He was the
One who could ascend into Heaven, even as the One
who was in Heaven. He is declaring that while in an
earthly form, He still had heavenly abilities. He is letting Nicodemus, and us know, this is what awakens in
us when we are born again.

As a result of us not knowing this, we haven't
experienced it. This means that everyone truly born
again has the capacities of the Spirit working in and
through them. They can encounter Heaven while
living on earth! As we develop these spiritual and
prophetic abilities through *"reason of use,"* Heaven
encounters are sure to come. Along with other
dimensions of Heaven, we will surely relate to and be
impacted by the Great Cloud of Witnesses.

Another safeguard that we should do to encounter these witnesses is **lay aside every weight and sin that would easily ensnare us.** Hebrews 12:1 zeros in on this requirement:

> *Therefore we also, since we are surrounded by so great a cloud of witnesses, let us lay aside every weight, and the sin which so easily ensnares us, and let us run with endurance the race that is set before us.*

Notice that because we are surrounded and have this spiritual activity around us, our awareness of this should make us live holier lives. For all those who would contradict we who believe in these things, I would say for them to examine the fruit of their lives. If they, in fact, believe what the Bible says about these things, it will press them to new places of purity and holiness. It will cause us to order our lives with a new commitment to sanctification. This will occur because we are aware of what we are living our lives in connection with. I believe as we do this, the Great Cloud of Witnesses is more apt to frequent our activities. This doesn't mean we are perfect. It does mean, however, that there is a passion to live holy. We will not be perfect until we either are in the Great Cloud of Witnesses ourselves or at Jesus' second coming when all things come to perfection.

Until that time, we are groaning within ourselves for these places and pressing into new realms of holiness and purity. The Cloud of Witnesses is drawn to that passion in us. In fact, the Cloud of Witnesses creates an atmosphere where a desire to lay our lives down is created. I have been in many meetings where the Cloud of Witnesses is sensed to be there with us. As they come in, the atmosphere of the room changes.

One pervasive occurrence is a passion to give our lives for Jesus' purpose is stirred. This is somewhat hard to explain, but we in the meeting become broken with this passion. This is because of the passion of those who are part of the Cloud of Witnesses. The atmosphere becomes pregnant with a heart to yield ourselves to God's will. We become empowered to offer our lives to Jesus.

Dreams—Spiritual Encounters

One of the most significant encounters I have had with this dimension was in a dream. Dreams are not always symbolic. They can be encounters in the spirit. In this dream, Ruth Heflin had appeared from the Cloud of Witnesses. If you do not know who Ruth Heflin is, she was instrumental in pioneering the "Glory Movement." The manifest presence of the Lord would move in her meetings with signs and wonders. She is considered by many to be the mother of this Glory Movement. Many trace their present-day ministries to her impact. Ruth passed away several years ago and has been in Heaven.

Before I tell you the dream, I must let you know I have never had any contact with Ruth Heflin. I was never in any of her meetings. I've never read any of her books. I never met her on any level. In other words, there is no familiarity or reason in the natural for me to dream about her. This is one of the reasons why this dream captured my attention.

In this dream, Ruth Heflin appeared from the Cloud of Witnesses. She appeared because she wanted to speak to me. There were others in the dream who came to get me to bring me to where she had appeared. When I arrived, I began to interact with her. As I interacted with her, she would physically manifest from the spirit realm more and more. Others would then try to interact with her. She would vanish or fade away as they would try to speak with her.

I had the distinct sense and understanding that the Cloud of Witnesses "liked" me and would respond to me. I jokingly say, "I may not have many friends on earth, but I do have ones in Heaven." As this scenario continued in the dream, Ruth began to prophesy over me. As she did, someone interrupted and said, "What about us?" They wanted a prophecy too. Ruth Heflin stopped and looked at this person and said with sternness in her voice, "It's Robert's turn." I knew she was saying, "He's been left out, passed over, disregarded, abused, and mistreated."

I awoke from the dream realizing I had just had a heavenly encounter. Since that time, great opportunities have opened up. Amazing doors continue to swing wide and God is granting new levels of influence and impact. I know these new opportunities were unlocked because of my encounter with Ruth Heflin in the Cloud of Witnesses. She wasn't just bringing a message from Heaven, she was through the prophetic releasing testimony before the Courts of Heaven. Her influence in Heaven was securing for me what others with influence on earth had been unwilling to grant.

I believe she and others from the Cloud of Witnesses have spoken on my behalf in the Courts of Heaven. Because they, from their life on earth, have received a *"good testimony,"* they have an influence in Heaven that has been granted them. Out of my understanding of the judicial system of Heaven, I began to agree with this testimony, or prophetic decree, of Ruth Heflin. In prayer I declare, "I agree with Ruth Heflin and the Cloud of Witnesses concerning my destiny. I proclaim, 'It is my turn.'" This comes from my awareness of the word "confession" in the Greek, which is the word *homologeo* and means agreeing testimony. When I confess, I am agreeing with Heaven's testimony. Agreeing testimony is very

The Cloud of Witnesses in the Courts of Heaven

important. God, from His judicial position as Judge, can only release verdicts based on more than one witness. Deuteronomy 19:15 gives us this standard:

> One witness shall not rise against a man concerning any iniquity or any sin that he commits; by the mouth of two or three witnesses the matter shall be established.

Apostle Paul also spoke of this in Second Corinthians 13:1:

> This will be the third time I am coming to you. "By the mouth of two or three witnesses every word shall be established."

Paul said there was a need for every word to be established by two or three witnesses. When we agree through confession with Heaven, we are pulling into earth Heaven's will. This is why I agree with what Ruth Heflin declared from the Cloud of Witnesses. Her testimony from the place she has been granted has great power when I agree with it here on earth! I want to be very clear that I am not praying to Ruth Heflin or any other person in the Cloud of Witnesses. I believe we pray to the Godhead only (Matthew 6:6). I can agree with the Cloud of Witnesses and their testimony, just like I agree with others on earth

(Matthew 18:19), It is the Father, Son, and even the Holy Spirit that my prayers are directed toward. The saints in the Cloud of Witnesses may be agreeing with my prayers, but I am not praying to them.

Another thought concerning guidelines, safeguards, to interacting with the Cloud of Witnesses and getting the benefit of their present-day function is *run with endurance our race of life.* Hebrews 12:1 connects the Cloud of Witnesses to our faithfulness and obedience:

> *Therefore we also, since we are surrounded*
> *by so great a cloud of witnesses, let us lay*
> *aside every weight, and the sin which so easily*
> *ensnares us, and let us run with endurance the*
> *race that is set before us.*

It seems the more faithful we are and the more we desire to obey, the more the witnesses can be part of strengthening us. I remember being in a service where the worship leader, who is also the senior pastor of church, began to sing from the Cloud of Witnesses a prophetic song. He began to sing as if the Cloud of Witnesses was singing it over us. He sang, "You're going to make it, you're going to cross the finish line." Literally as he sang this, the atmosphere changed. The glory of God entered the room. The weight of

God's person seemed to inundate us. It was an awesome time.

I believe the Cloud of Witnesses was, in fact, singing over us and bringing us strength for our race. As he sang, fear, guilt, unworthiness, shame, and everything that would whisper we weren't going to make it and finish, dropped away. We were receiving strength from the Cloud of Witnesses. Quite often it seemed, the Cloud of Witnesses came into a service and began to empower us. Actually, more correctly, I believe we "come to" where they are in a dimension of the spirit (Hebrews 12:24).

I believe as we connect, they pray and prophesy over us as we need new power and might to finish. It is ultimately the strength of the Lord but it is being administered and ministered through the "spirits of just men made perfect." Who said they lose this ministry just because they go to Heaven. They are still part of the family of God in Heaven and on earth. Therefore, *God can use them to minister His life into us*.

Much of the function and operation of the Great Cloud of Witnesses is a mystery. We at best can get glimpses from Scripture of what they are doing as it relates to us on earth. I do not believe that God will violate the Scripture as we know it. I, however, also believe that the Holy Spirit teaches us all things and will guide us into all truth (John 16:13). Along with the truth of Scripture, we must also pay attention to what the Holy Spirit is bearing witness. First John 2:26-27 tells us that the Holy Spirit will teach us and keep us from being seduced:

> *These things I have written to you concerning those who try to deceive you. But the anointing which you have received from Him abides in you, and you do not need that anyone teach you; but as the same anointing teaches you concerning all things, and is true, and is not a lie, and just as it has taught you, you will abide in Him.*

Apostle John said coupled with the word he had taught them, the anointing or Holy Spirit would help them recognize truth and lies. We should, along with the Word of God, learn to pay attention to what the Spirit is approving or disapproving. If we don't learn to do this, we can become legalistic and miss supernatural encounters God has for us.

There are realms of the spirit we are to interact with. May we have the wisdom to not disregard them just because they are unfamiliar. We might dismiss something meant to empower our lives and change our future.

Chapter 7

Encountering the Cloud of Witnesses

AS you can tell by now, I believe fully in a spiritual dimension where the Cloud of Witnesses is active and even involved in our lives. I have had many different encounters with this realm. I've only shared a handful of them. As we finish this book, I want to point out a few more functions I see the Cloud of Witnesses involved in. In Revelation 19:10, we see John having an encounter with a heavenly being:

> And I fell at his feet to worship him. But he said to me, "See that you do not do that! I am your **fellow servant,** and of **your brethren** who have the testimony of Jesus. Worship God! For the **testimony of Jesus** is the spirit of prophecy."

As we traditionally read this verse, we would think John is having an encounter with an angel. Upon closer investigation though, we might come to a different conclusion. John falls to worship this entity. This is probably why we assume this is an angel. He has such glory on him that John feels compelled to worship. He is told, however, not to. Worship belongs only to the Lord.

Heaven is jealous for Jesus and the Godhead to get all the worship and all the glory. This being then makes some statements that can give us clues to who he is and where he's from. First of all, he declares, "I am your fellow servant." He doesn't say, "I'm your servant." If this is what he said, then he might be an angel because they are our servants sent to minister to the heirs of salvation (Hebrews 1:14). He, however, says he is John's *"**fellow** servant."* This means he is like us. He is of human form. Angels actually are not of human form. Ultimately, we will judge them. First Corinthians 6:2-3 reveals that we will judge angels in the life to come:

> *Do you not know that the saints will judge the world? And if the world will be judged by you, are you unworthy to judge the smallest matters? Do you not know that **we shall judge angels**? How much more, things that pertain to this life?*

There is a distinct difference in rank between angels and humans. This entity claiming to be John's fellow servant could not be an angel. He is saying he is just like us.

A second clue about this entity is found in his statement that he is John's brother. Angels are not our brothers. That would mean we have the same DNA and can operate the same way. It would mean we have the same nature. This is not true. Presently angels have been given a higher ranking than humans. Psalm 8:4-5 states that presently angels and humans operate in two different spheres:

What is man that You are mindful of him, and the son of man that You visit him? For You have made him a little lower than the angels, and You have crowned him with glory and honor.

Right now, we are lower than angels in rank. This means we are two different species. We are not brothers. Later we will be higher than the angels because as we saw, we will judge them. At no time, however, are we equal to them. This is because we are not "brothers" with angels. This being John is encountering claims, however, to be his brother. This would mean he is not an angel.

Another clue is that this being claims to have the *"testimony of Jesus."* The testimony of Jesus means they carry in their spirit the revelation of who Jesus is and can give witness to it from a firsthand account. We are told in First Peter 1:10-12 that angels desire to look into the salvation granted us:

> *Of this salvation the prophets have inquired and searched carefully, who prophesied of the grace that would come to you, searching what, or what manner of time, the Spirit of Christ who was in them was indicating when He testified before-hand the sufferings of Christ and the glories that would follow. To them it was revealed that, not to themselves, but to us they were ministering the things which now have been reported to you through those who have preached the gospel to you by the Holy Spirit sent from heaven—things which **angels desire to look into.***

The prophets prophesied of the salvation that we would have. The Spirit of Christ was in them showing the suffering Jesus would go through centuries and millenniums before it occurred. These prophets could "see" what was coming. Notice that the angels desired to look into all this but were forbidden. They could not see and have the testimony of Jesus that would bring them to salvation. This is why there is no redemption for the angels that fell. Only for humankind did Jesus die.

Angels are unredeemable. They are not human and salvation is not for them. This is why this being that John is encountering cannot be an angel. He, in fact, claims to have the testimony of Jesus. All of this would make him only one thing, human! This would mean he is from the Great Cloud of Witnesses. He is not an angel, he is of human form on assignment from God. The question would be asked, "If he is human, why would John fall to worship him?" The answer would be because he no longer has the veil of the flesh shielding the glory that is in him.

The truth is, we don't know who we really are and what dwells in us. In Colossians 1:26-27 we see Paul explaining what is in us:

> The **mystery** which has been hidden from
> ages and from generations, but now has been
> **revealed to His saints**. To them God willed to
> make known what are the riches of the glory of
> this mystery among the Gentiles: which is **Christ
> in you, the hope of glory**.

Paul said this was a mystery—something unknown and hidden. It is Christ in us the hope of glory. The One who lives in us is more glorious than we can imagine. We carry this glory in our spirits. Should this veil of the flesh be removed, we would be astounded at who we really are as a result of Jesus in us! This is why John falls to worship this guy. He is overwhelmed by the glory associated with him. This glory is in us now. We just don't realize it. If we did, we would be so much bolder and filled with faith.

There is a glory in us that overcomes the world and defeats any and every enemy. This is why John fell to worship, but was told not to. In essence he was told, "Don't worship me, the same glory is in you, you just don't know it. Worship God!"

Clearly this heavenly being is not an angel. I believe this is a human person from the Cloud of Witnesses. This is the only other option. This brings up all sorts of other questions. Although the main one is, "Are people from the Cloud of Witnesses allowed functions and assignments to people who are yet on earth?" It would appear so. This person is unveiling mysteries to John about the spiritual dimension and how things work in the heavenly realm. Could it be that God uses people from the Cloud of Witnesses to help us understand spiritual mysteries? Heresy you say. Then what are we to do with the reality of these Scriptures? Or maybe we need to be challenged to think outside our religious box and realize there are realms of the spirit we might need to encounter. May God help us and grant us wisdom in these matters. This person from the Great Cloud of Witnesses is giving John understanding of mysteries yet unfolded. Even so, these mysteries are still being revealed and unveiled through the anointing of the Spirit. One distinctive of all the heavenly hosts, be it the angels or the spirits of just people made perfect, is that they are marked by the glory of God. In that realm, they have access to dimensions of the glory of God that we have tasted of in part, and thus, they are still functioning out of that glory.

God Uses Witnesses

One other encounter I have had with the Cloud of Witnesses concerns my wife, Mary. As I was away on a ministry trip, I had a very powerful dream where Mary's Aunt Mildred appeared to me. Mary was standing before me in my dream. Standing behind her was her aunt, Mildred. Mildred passed away quite a few years ago. Mary is saying to me in the dream, "I'm getting stronger and stronger." She is saying this in regard to her physical being. As she says this, Aunt Mildred stands with her arms folded. She begins to shake her head in disagreement. She doesn't say anything, but I know she is saying, "No, she is getting weaker and weaker and will die prematurely."

I awake from the dream knowing that Aunt Mildred has been allowed from the Cloud of Witnesses to communicate the intent of the devil against my wife. I knew there was a scheme of the devil to take out the women of Mary's bloodline prematurely. This dream caused us to deal with issues in the bloodline of Mary that would allow this history to continue. As a result, we have from the Courts of Heaven secured the long and satisfying life God has promised (Psalm 91:16). The information, however, came as a result of someone from the Cloud of Witnesses. God can use them for different errands and assignments from their heavenly place.

I want to point out one final thing concerning the function of the Cloud of Witnesses. When you realize that Hebrews 11 is describing the saints of faith and what qualifies them to be in this Cloud of Witnesses, it beckons us to examine from this viewpoint. These all walked in obedience, sacrifice, self-surrender, and faithfulness to the call of God. However, the one factor driving all of them was faith. It was their faith that allowed the kind of life to be lived that has now secured them their heavenly realm and function. Heaven places a strong premium on faith!

Remember, it was their faith that actually declares them just (Romans 1:17). Their faith in that which was yet to come brought them to being the spirits of just men made perfect. This means that their presence will challenge us to new realms of faith. Hebrews 11:2 tells us that the elders obtained a good testimony because of their faith:

For by it the elders obtained a good testimony.

Who are these elders? I know others may not agree, but the Bible says there are 24 elders sitting on 24 thrones in Heaven. They are part of a celestial council. Revelation 4:4 shows us these elders sitting on their thrones:

> *Around the throne were twenty-four thrones, and on the thrones I saw twenty-four elders sitting, clothed in white robes; and they had crowns of gold on their heads.*

Could it be that these have this place of a "good testimony" and status in Heaven because of their faith? It was their faith that secured this position and function in Heaven? The bottom line is clearly, Heaven loves it when we walk by a faith that even causes us to lay down our lives for His Kingdom. This is what the Great Cloud of Witnesses did and what we are to do as well. So what does it mean to live by faith?

Living by Faith

Living by faith means I order my life by the Word of God more than human philosophy. I am willing to lay down my life where the Word of God demands something of me that doesn't agree with the spirit of this age. I choose the ways of the Lord rather than conventional wisdom when it disagrees with God's revealed ideas. This is what the Great Cloud of Witnesses did. Hebrews 11:24-26 shows that Moses forsook Egypt and its ways for the ways of God:

> By faith Moses, when he became of age, refused to be called the son of Pharaoh's daughter, choosing rather to suffer affliction with the people of God than to enjoy the passing pleasures of sin, esteeming the reproach of Christ greater riches than the treasures in Egypt; for he looked to the reward.

Moses chose by faith the reproaching of Christ rather than selling out to the treasures of Egypt. He had a revelation he lived his life from. Christ was not yet born, yet Moses by revelation could see the unseen. This caused him to sacrifice the comfort of Egypt for the reward he could only see in the spirit. His obedience secured him a great place in the Cloud of Witnesses.

Living by faith is also believing what you can't see more than what you can see! This is what Abraham did. Hebrews 11:8 tells us Abraham left everything to chase something he couldn't see naturally:

*By faith Abraham obeyed when he was called to
go out to the place which he would receive as an
inheritance. And* **he went out, not knowing
where he was going**.

At the very core of faith, we must be willing to
live more by what we sense in the spirit rather than
what we see in the natural. This is what is meant by
the declaration we *"live by faith and not by sight."* Second Corinthians 5:7 tells us this is the normal for us
as spiritual people:

For we walk by faith, not by sight.

The more we serve God, the more the faith realm
of operating in the unseen becomes comfortable to us.
We begin to know by experience that the unseen is just
as real as what we can see. We also become convinced
that the spiritual realm controls the natural realm. This
is what the Cloud of Witnesses functions in.

Living by faith is also using our faith to win great
victories in the natural. Hebrews 11:32-35 lists natural things that happened because normal people
stepped into the faith realm:

*And what more shall I say? For the time would
fail me to tell of Gideon and Barak and Samson*

*and Jephthah, also of David and Samuel and
the prophets: who through faith subdued kingdoms, worked righteousness, obtained promises,
stopped the mouths of lions, quenched the vio-
lence of fire, escaped the edge of the sword, out
of weakness were made strong, became valiant
in battle, turned to flight the armies of the aliens.
Women received their dead raised to life again.
Others were tortured, not accepting deliverance,
that they might obtain a better resurrection.*

This is a list of feats and accomplishments of
those who used faith to gain victories and expand the
rule of the kingdom. As a result, they obtained a great
place in Heaven in the Cloud of Witnesses. Their
faith secured victories and breakthroughs on earth
but also granted placement in Heaven. First John 5:4
tells us that our faith wins victories:

*For whatever is born of God overcomes the
world. And this is **the victory that has overcome the world—our faith.***

These are not just victories for us personally. God
would have us use our faith to win victories to expand
His Kingdom influence on the earth. Everything we
accomplish on earth for God is done through faith.
This requires some form of laying our lives down to

see it happen. Real faith will cause us to sacrifice our own life for the will of the Kingdom. The more we choose this, the more we are securing for ourselves a good testimony. This allows us a function in the Courts of Heaven now, but also a place in Heaven's Court in the next life.

We can be among those who would be part of the Cloud of Witnesses to allow God's will to be done on earth until the fullness of all things. May we continually learn to connect to our spiritual heritage of those who are in the Cloud of Witnesses. May we walk by faith and not by sight and win for ourselves a placement in Heaven alongside those already there. The life of faith is greatly rewarded in this life and the one to come. May we agree with all the activity of Heaven by faith, including the Great Cloud of Witnesses that Heaven may invade earth!

Have you ever wondered about the saints who watch us from the grandstands of Heaven? How about *the powers of the coming age* that are mentioned in the Bible as well? I have asked the Lord for understanding on these two subjects. The *powers of the coming age* and *the Great Cloud of Witnesses* are both mentioned in the book of Hebrews:

*For it is impossible for those who were once
enlightened, and have tasted the heavenly gift,
and have become partakers of the Holy Spirit,
and have tasted the good word of God and **the
powers of the age to come**, if they fall away,
to renew them again to repentance, since they
crucify again for themselves the Son of God, and
put Him to an open shame (Hebrews 6:4-6).*

*Therefore we also, since we are surrounded
by so **great a crowd of witnesses,** let us lay
aside every weight, and the sin which so easily
ensnares us, and let us run with endurance the
race that is set before us (Hebrews 12:1).*

I always wondered what the Lord meant when He
spoke of the powers of the age to come and the Cloud
of Witnesses. I asked the Lord, "What are the powers
of the coming age?" The Word says that we've experienced the powers of coming age. I wondered about all
the men and women of God who had walked in this
power before me who are now in the Great Cloud of
Witnesses. It is so important to understand that many
saints stand in agreement in the courts of Heaven
with you in order to complete your destiny in God for
this generation.

So I began to intensely seek the Lord for understanding of these passages of Scripture. The Lord answered me with an amazing encounter:

The encounter occurred on October 16, 2012, on my wife's birthday. Kathi and I were on an airplane traveling to Seattle. I had put on my headset and was relaxing after flying for several days during my job with an airline. I was sitting in an aisle seat and someone came and stood beside me in the aisle. I opened my eyes and the power of God overcame me. Initially, I did not see anybody. But suddenly, I saw an angel standing in the aisle beside me. He grabbed me and took me away.

We left the airplane in a vision. We traveled very quickly. He had me by the arm, and away we went. We landed where there was a forest that opened to a field. I did not know where we were. I saw a man who was quite short. He was walking on the path in front of us. He wore a garment that reminded me of an animal skin.

The angel spoke, "I've been given permission to show you the powers of the coming age." He said, "Watch!" He pointed to the man as he took one more step. The resurrection power just burst around him as he stepped from the earthly realm into the heavenly realm. His name was Enoch.

The power that came out from him as he stepped into the heavenly realm was extremely strong. That power overtook both the angel and me. The power burst right through us, and its presence was bright and intensely strong. Then the angel said, "Come." He took me and we went to another place very quickly. I saw another man standing. It was Elijah. A chariot came, and he got in it. The same thing happened— there was a sudden burst of resurrection power. The same power that raised Jesus from the dead, burst around him, and Elijah disappeared. The blast came back and hit us once again. It was so strong!

Then the angel turned to me and handed me a scroll. I do not have the scroll because it was a scroll that was from that event that was happening at the time. It was an event found in Bible. He said, "You need to read Second Corinthians, chapter 5, especially verse 17. You have been called to a ministry of reconciliation." The angel explained, "You have been shown the powers of the coming age so you can participate in it right now."

He said, "People need to be told that they have been bought and purchased, that all of humanity has been bought and purchased. They need to be told that the price has already been paid. You tell them that God has purchased them through Jesus Christ, and this is the powers of the coming age." He then took me back to 40,000 feet, put me in my seat on the right side of the airplane, and left.

I realized that the resurrection power that is dwelling in me wants to raise people from the dead. I can spiritually raise people from the dead just by testifying of Jesus. Testifying of Christ initiates that resurrection power. It's a function of the ministry of reconciliation. The angel had given me a scroll, but I did not have it when I returned. The scroll had contained the entire fifth chapter of Second Corinthians, which the angel said I needed to learn. He said, "You need to learn the whole chapter."

On different occasions, during visitations in Heaven, I have encountered other saints of God from the Cloud of Witnesses who have encouraged me in the walk of power and ministry similar to that of Elijah and Enoch. These particular saints know God's plan for this present generation. They know we are included in this powerful ministry and that we must walk in the spirit of revelation presently. Saints who are in the Cloud of Witnesses, whom we may admire, are actually excited to meet us because of our importance in these last days. We are chosen vessels in the final move and revelation of God's glory.

It is the ministry of reconciliation! The resurrection power is so strong that when someone testifies, that testimony raises people from the dead spiritually.

People come back to life right before your eyes as you announce this Good News to them. The Lord explained to me why it is that the testimony of Jesus is the Spirit of Prophecy:

> *And I fell at his feet to worship him. But he said to me, "See that you do not do that! I am your fellow servant, and of your brethren who have the testimony of Jesus. Worship God! For the testimony of Jesus is the spirit of prophecy"* (Revelation 19:10).

In these last days, the veil between the heavenly realm and this earthly realm has, in a sense, become thin as we begin to encounter the fulfillment of God's heart for the ages. When people start to talk about Jesus, their words begin to turn into *prophecy— because the Spirit wants to testify and take over.* When a person starts talking about Jesus, the Holy Spirit automatically manifests every time. I can almost hear the cheers of all who have selflessly labored and gone on before us. They are shouting, "Be encouraged and run your race with fervency!" (see Hebrews 12:2).

—Kevin L. Zadai, ThD

Chapter 8

Jesus, the Mediator

AS we finish our thoughts on the Great Cloud of Witnesses, I want to reemphasize once again that *it's all about Jesus*. It doesn't matter what encounter we might have, what doctrine we are excited about, or what gift or visitation we have, if these things do not press us and push us to new levels of love and passion for Jesus, we should run from them. Anything that is truly out of the heavenly realm will have this effect. Colossians 1:17-18 tells us that Jesus is preeminent:

And He is before all things, and in Him all things consist. And He is the head of the body, the church, who is the beginning, the firstborn from the dead, that in all things He may have the preeminence.

The passion the Father has for the Son has caused Him to give Him a name above every other name.

Philippians 2:9-10 shows that God has highly exalted Jesus and His name:

> *Therefore God also has highly exalted Him and*
> *given Him the name which is above every name,*
> *that at the name of Jesus every knee should bow,*
> *of those in heaven, and of those on earth, and of*
> *those under the earth.*

Only at the name of Jesus will knees bow and tongues confess He is Lord. In the midst of any and all spiritual encounters, I must ask, "Is this pushing me to Jesus and glorifying His name?" If it isn't, it is to be avoided. Jesus alone is the Savior of the world. Any godly spiritual encounter will reinforce His sovereignty and give honor to Him. Apostle Peter declared that only the name of Jesus has salvation in it. Peter says in Acts 4:11-12 says there is salvation only in the name of Jesus and no other:

> *This is the "stone which was rejected by you*
> *builders, which has become the chief corner-*
> *stone." Nor is there salvation in any other,*
> *for there is no other name under heaven given*
> *among men by which we must be saved.*

Thank the Lord for the name of Jesus. At His name the spirit world and the natural world will respond. There is absolute power in His name. We are also told in Revelation 1:7-8 of Jesus' preeminence:

> *Behold, He is coming with clouds, and every eye will see Him, even they who pierced Him. And all the tribes of the earth will mourn because of Him. Even so, Amen. "I am the Alpha and the Omega, the Beginning and the End," says the Lord, "who is and who was and who is to come, the Almighty."*

Jesus, in revealing Himself to John, declares that He is the Alpha, Omega, the Beginning and the End. This means among other things that He is before all things, He is after all things, and is everything in between. There can never be too much emphasis placed on who Jesus is. Only by Him, through Him, and with Him is there life and salvation. This is why Paul declares that if any other gospel was preached, then let them be accursed. Galatians 1:8-9 shows that even if spiritual encounters come that seem to be legitimate, if they take away from the gospel of Jesus Christ, we should flee from it:

> *But even if we, or an angel from heaven, preach any other gospel to you than what we have preached to you, let him be accursed. As we have said before, so now I say again, if anyone*

preaches any other gospel to you than what you
have received, let him be accursed.

Notice that Paul speaks of angelic visitation from
Heaven. He also speaks of himself as an apostle. He
declares that only the gospel of Jesus Christ is to be
accepted and embraced. Any supernatural encounter
that would detract from this must be judged as false
and deceptive. Of course, we know and realize that
Jesus said this about Himself in John 14:6. He alone is
the way, the truth, and the life:

Jesus said to him, "I am the way, the truth,
and the life. No one comes to the Father except
through Me."

Only through and by Jesus do we come to the
Father and obtain resurrected life and power. We
must always keep Jesus at the front and center of all
spiritual experiences and encounters.

Having said this, I believe there are spiritual realities in Heaven that are part of the intercessory ministry of Jesus. We know Jesus is praying for us at the
right hand of the Father. Romans 8:34 tells us of Jesus'
intercession on our behalf at the right hand of God:

*Who is he who condemns? It is Christ who died,
and furthermore is also risen, who is even at the
right hand of God, who also makes intercession
for us.*

Jesus is praying for us. What a glorious thought
that even though He died on the Cross, He is still
active on our behalf. I believe Revelation 19:10
reveals that this intercession is considered the testimony of Jesus. Jesus from His position as Intercessor
in the heavenlies is actually operating in a judicial
place:

*And I fell at his feet to worship him. But he said
to me, "See that you do not do that! I am your
fellow servant, and of your brethren who have
the **testimony of Jesus.** Worship God! For the
testimony of Jesus is the spirit of prophecy."*

The Bible calls this the *"testimony of Jesus,"* not
the testimony about Jesus. In other words, this is the
testimony Jesus is presently releasing before the throne
of God on our behalf. This sets things in judicial order
for God's will to be done in us and through us. That
testimony becomes a spirit of prophecy or a prophetic
unction that we as His people pray in harmony with
Him. This is where we begin to intercede with the

same passion Jesus is carrying before the throne of God on behalf of God's purposes being done.

What an amazing honor the Lord has granted us to stand in such a holy function and place. This is why the apostle Paul spoke of intercession being made for all people in First Timothy 2:1:

> *Therefore I exhort first of all that supplications, prayers, intercessions, and giving of thanks be made for all men.*

Intercession is one of four types of prayers Paul mentions here. Intercession in the Greek is the word *enteuxis* and it means an interview. But when you look at it deeper, you discover the word it comes from is *entugchano* and means to chance upon, to confer with. This means that during our times of prayer, the Spirit of God, or the prophetic unction, can take the intercession or testimony Jesus is giving before the throne and cause us to partake of it. This is the testimony of Jesus being the Spirit of Prophecy. This isn't about prophesying per say as much as it is about a prophetic unction to pray from. At times it seems to chance upon us seemingly out of the blue. When this happens, we are able to agree with what our Intercessor Jesus is doing on behalf of God's passion before the throne.

Furthermore, the Great Cloud of Witnesses also agrees with Jesus' prayers because they have this testimony as well. Remember that they are witnesses. This means those who give judicial testimony. If Jesus' testimony is in fact intercession before God's presence, then the witness of the Cloud of Witnesses is also intercession.

They are also agreeing with the prayers of Jesus at the throne of God. They also stand as an extension of His intercession on behalf of God's passion on earth.

It doesn't, however, stop there. We also know the blood of Jesus is speaking. According to Hebrews 12:24, the blood is speaking and releasing testimony in the Courts of Heaven:

> *To Jesus the Mediator of the new covenant, and to the blood of sprinkling that speaks better things than that of Abel.*

Just like the testimony of Abel's blood caused God to judge Cain, the blood of Jesus grants God the legal right to forgive, redeem, and remember us. So the blood of Jesus is also releasing testimony and intercession on our behalf as well.

There is One more who is also agreeing with the intercession of Jesus—the Holy Spirit. Romans 8:26-27 tells us of these groanings of the Spirit of God:

*Likewise the Spirit also helps in our weaknesses.
For we do not know what we should pray for as
we ought, but the Spirit Himself makes intercession for us with groanings which cannot be
uttered. Now He who searches the hearts knows
what the mind of the Spirit is, because He makes
intercession for the saints according to the will of
God.*

In agreement with Jesus' intercession and testimony, the Holy Spirit is groaning for His passion to
be fulfilled. Sometimes the groanings of the Spirit are
poured through us as the Spirit agrees with the cry of
Jesus' heart as Intercessor.

My point in all of this is, there is much activity
in Heaven. It all, however, flows out of Jesus and His
passion, desire, and purpose. Jesus is the center of all
things. As we are fully established and aware of this,
we may encounter all this activity I have mentioned
and even more.

The Great Cloud of Witnesses is part of this activity of Heaven. They are always carrying out the passion of Jesus and His desires. May the same Spirit and
desire that is in them, be in us as we lay down our lives
with them, for Jesus' will to be done on earth. We are
here alongside them to see Jesus' passion fulfilled. As

the Moravian's sang and declared, "We are here to win for the Lord the rewards of His sufferings."

So be it, Lord Jesus!

About the Author

ROBERT HENDERSON is a global apostolic leader who operates in revelation and impartation. His teaching empowers the Body of Christ to see the hidden truths of Scripture clearly and apply them for breakthrough results. Driven by a mandate to disciple nations through writing and speaking, Robert travels extensively around the globe teaching on the apostolic, the Kingdom of God, the "Seven Mountains," and most notably, the Courts of Heaven. He and his wife, Mary, have been married for more than years and they have six children and five grandchildren. Together they are enjoying life in beautiful Midlothian, Texas.

INCREASE THE EFFECTIVENESS OF YOUR PRAYERS.

Learn how to release your destiny from Heaven's Courts!

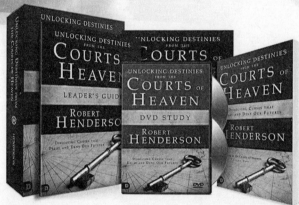

Unlocking Destinies from the Courts of Heaven

Curriculum Box Set Includes:
9 Video Teaching Sessions (2 DVD Disks), Unlocking Destinies book,
Interactive Manual, Leader's Guide

There are books in Heaven that record your destiny and purpose. Their pages describe the very reason you were placed on the Earth.

And yet, there is a war against destiny being fulfilled. Your archenemy, the devil, knows that as you occupy your divine assignment, by default, the powers of darkness are demolished. Heaven comes to Earth as God's people fulfill their Kingdom callings!

In The *Unlocking Destinies from the Courts of Heaven* book and curriculum, Robert Henderson takes you step by step through a prophetic prayer strategy. By watching the powerful video sessions and going through the Courts of Heaven process using the interactive manual, you will learn how to dissolve the delays and hindrances to your destiny being fulfilled.